KW-333-337

Past-into-Present Series

FACTORIES

R. A. S. Hennessey

Head of the Economics Department
at the Royal Grammar School, Newcastle Upon Tyne

LIVERPOOL COLLEGE OF ART

B. T. BATSFORD LTD LONDON

First published 1969
© R. A. S. Hennessey, 1969

Filmset by Keyspools Ltd, Golborne, Lancashire

Printed and bound in Italy
by Officine Fotolitografiche, S.P.A.. Casarile, Milano

By the same author
Transport

LIVERPOOL REGIONAL
COLLEGE OF ART

Acc. No. 69/740

Class No. 725.4

Copy

Rebound

Gen

Acknowledgment

The author and publishers would like to thank the following for permission to reproduce the illustrations appearing in this book: Airviews Ltd., Manchester, for fig. 64; Associated Electrical Industries Ltd. for fig. 58; Amalgamated Engineering Union for fig. 33; Associated Iliffe Press for figs. 37 and 38; A. Banks, Esq., Surrey Art Designs, for figs. 4 and 8; D. B. Barton, Esq., Truro, for figs. 16 and 25; The Bowater Organisation for figs. 40 and 41; The British Motor Corporation Ltd. for fig. 70; Dorman Long (Steel) Ltd. for fig. 32; Electricity Generating Board for figs. 66, 67 and 68; Ford's, Dagenham, for fig. 71; Imperial Chemical Industries Ltd. for figs. 46, 47 and 48; Imperial War Museum for fig. 36; The Controller, H.M. Stationery Office, for figs. 59 and 60; Literary and Philosophical Society of Newcastle Upon Tyne for fig. 14; Manchester Art Gallery for fig. 53; Mansell Collection for figs. 3, 5, 6, 7, 10, 11, 17, 18, 19, 20, 21, 23, 24, 34, 35, 50, 52, 54 and 56; National Film Archive for fig. 61; National Museum of Wales for fig. 13; North Thames Gas Board for fig. 31; Oldham Public Libraries for figs. 30 and 57; Radio Times Hulton Picture Library for figs. 9, 15, 29, 42, 51, 55, 63 and 69; C. J. Rainford, A.R.I.B.A., for fig. 2; Miss K. Ritson for fig. 28; Royal Institute of British Architects for fig. 65; The Trustees of the Tate Gallery for fig. 62; Unilever Merseyside Ltd. for fig. 49; E. J. D. Warrilow, Esq., for fig. 12; Westburn Sugar Refineries for fig. 26; and W. D. & H. O. Wills Ltd. for figs. 44 and 45. Other sources are indicated in the captions.

Contents

The Illustrations

Introduction: The Factory

The *Oxford English Dictionary* defines a factory as: 'Merchant's or factor's trading station in a foreign country' or: 'A building or group of buildings where articles of commerce are manufactured'. The first usage is now out of date, as is the kind of institution which it describes. But in the eighteenth century the first was widely used, whereas the second meaning was virtually unknown. This was, quite simply, because factories as we know them were only just beginning. Men could hardly have guessed that this late intruder into economic life—which had gone on for some 8,000 years without it—was to dominate civilisation within a hundred years.

Until that time manufacture had taken place in two ways: by the *domestic* or cottage system, whereby people made things in their own homes; or in *work-shops* where a number of craftsmen gathered in one place. The factory, as shown in Chapter 1, required certain elements only available from the mid-eighteenth century onwards, e.g. efficient machinery, big markets, large quantities of investible wealth, good communications. Walter James, writing in the magazine *Progress*, the Unilever quarterly, said: 'I should like to take young historians to the edge of the moors in Lancashire on a clear day and say to them "Look down there among the chimneys; there, in the corner of your own country, the modern world began".'

This book attempts to explain the origin, location and effects of factories on British society and civilisation. Sometimes factories are known by other names in certain industries; thus there are cotton 'mills'; ship 'yards'; gas 'works'; and power 'stations'. They are all, from an economic point of view, factories. This book also deals with mines, because modern mining, like modern manufacturing, dates from the eighteenth century, developed in the same way and had similarly profound effects on society. These effects are dealt with in the second part of the book: the first describes the spread of the factory system to various industries.

Note on comparative money values: figures relating to sums of money in past history have to be adjusted if they are to compare with prices in 1969. £1 in 1967 would only buy the equivalent of 2s. 11d. in 1900, and far less in 1800.

LIVERPOOL COLLEGE OF ART

1 The Dawn of the Factory Age

'Those unsightly chimneys and that disfiguring smoke are a most wholesome balance to the palace and gardens of Wentworth. Were it not for them England would be no better than Russia or Poland—we should be the mere serfs of a territorial aristocracy.' This was the opinion of Dr Arnold, the headmaster of Rugby School and an acute observer of society in his day, the 1830s in this case. Like the railways which he also welcomed, the factories were symbols of a new age and a new civilisation.

In the history of man, there have been two basic economic revolutions. The first was the discovery of agriculture, about 7000 BC. This enabled man to settle and become civilised in a way that would be unlikely in a hunting or nomadic society. The other was the Industrial Revolution, beginning about 1780 onwards, which released men from the land and offered work in factories. Society became urban, i.e. town-based, and was able, in due course, to offer a higher standard of living to the bulk of its members. Thus human society has been peopled by hunters and farmers for most of its history, and the industrial world in which we live is very recent in origin.

Like Dr Arnold, many of his contemporaries sensed that industrialism was revolutionary. The French publicist, Louis Blanqui, first used the term 'Industrial Revolution' in 1837. It brought a civilisation so different from any previously known, that pre-industrial society might almost have existed on a different planet. Instead of toiling in fields, men worked in factories or offices; or in mines or mills. In place of rural villages there grew immense and gloomy industrial cities: Birmingham, Essen, Charleroi and Pittsburgh. In all this there was, however, a hope. Pre-industrial, or agrarian, society supported a thin crust of people in affluence and luxury: the nobility, gentry and some of the middle class of ports and towns. Industrial society made it possible for all to share, albeit unequally, in greater luxury. For instance, owning a car or a television is now fairly commonplace in Western society. Two hundred years ago the life of the average member of society was poor and coarse, with little hope of anything better. This is an economic fact; the question of human happiness, satisfaction etc. in relation to an improving material standard of living is highly interesting, but it is beyond the scope of history.

By the 1830s new social classes were being created by these changes: a large industrial working class (or *proletariat*) and a middle class (or *bourgeoisie*) of managers, factory owners, clerks—the white collar workers of economic journalism. These classes were to dominate society and become the beneficiaries of industrialism.

1 The windmill at Eye, near Peterborough, built *c.* 1830 with brickworks chimneys in the background. This mill (which once sported the unusual number of eight sails) ground flour, as did most of Britain's 10,000 mills. Some 2,500, however, were used to pump and drain the Fens. Watermills, and even Tidemills, were used to obtain industrial energy in the pre-steam era. Windmills in Britain date from the twelfth century, but few remain today.

The Factory System

There were many general causes for these profound changes. The junction at which they all met and had effect was the Factory System. Factory production is (in economic terms) where an *entrepreneur* (organiser, or business man) hires *labour* to work machines (*capital*) in a building (also capital). The building will be erected on land and will process raw materials, such as cotton, iron, coal etc. which have been grown on or extracted from the *land*. *Land, labour* and *capital* are therefore called the 'Factors of Production'—the entrepreneur assimilates them. No factory system is possible unless the factors of production are readily available and can be intelligently related to each other.

It might be argued that a windmill (**1**) or cottage-dwelling family producing cloth before industrial times, satisfied the bare jargon of economists as to what constituted a factory. But the unique quality of a factory is scale. The factory system produced goods in large—even gigantic—quantities. It did this because it made possible the *division of labour*: a system whereby workers tend to do one component task in the stream of production rather than being 'Jacks of all trades, masters of none' which was often a feature of domestic industry. Specialisation makes a labourer more efficient and productive.

Workers were now occupied in tending spinning machines, boring cylinders,

TRAFFIC & SERVICE ZONE

DELIVERY
&
DESPATCH

OVERHEAD CONVEYORS

2 The archetype light factory: this was specially designed to house virtually any light industrial process since its size and shape can be altered if required. Heavy industry (steel, coal) usually

assembling components—and nothing else. If the factory had intense division of labour it became possible to indulge in mass-production: making goods of a standard type in vast quantities, be it cotton yarn, baked beans or the famous (and first) mass-produced car, the Model T Ford. The final stage, to date, is to construct machines to supervise the running of the factory itself; this is *automation*.

All these developments require special buildings in order to function efficiently. Jumbled workshops, cramped cottages or converted barns (a makeshift employed in the early factory age) are quite inadequate. The only environment in which advanced industrial methods can take place is the factory: an industrial building specially designed as such (**2**).

There has been much argument about what may be called the 'first factory'. Factories of a kind existed before industrial times (see pp. 15 and 50) such as the water-powered fulling mills which helped in the finishing process of woollen cloth production and were to be found from the twelfth century onwards, or the large breweries erected in great towns such as the one which inspired Sir William Brereton at Edinburgh (1634): 'I took notice here of that common brewhouse which supplies the whole city with beer and ale, and observed there the greatest, vastest leads . . . cisterns and combs (tubs) that ever I saw: the leads to cool the liquor were as large as a whole house.' A town tannery or soapworks was not unusual, but the element of technical ingenuity and elaboration was missing.

A good claim has been advanced on behalf of the Lombe brothers' six-storey silk factory erected near Derby (1718), containing advanced machinery and employing 300 workers. It was the wonder of its age, of which Daniel Defoe wrote (in his *A Tour through the Whole Island of Great Britain*, 1727): 'A curiosity of a very extraordinary nature', and went on to wax enthusiastically about its '22,586 wheels . . . which work 73,726 yards of silk in twenty-four hours'. Although his delight is rather spent in mathematical exactitude, one can share his sense of novelty.

AXE LTD.

PEDESTRIAN ZONE

DEMOUNTABLE GALLERY AS REQUIRED

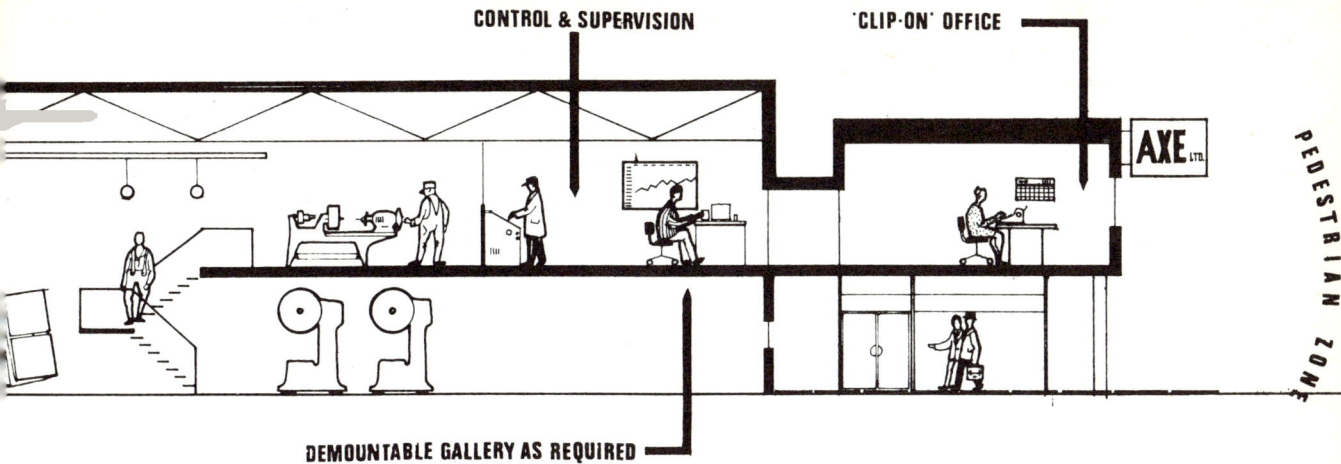

needs special buildings and plant. Lighter industries are less exacting in their needs, hence the move to standard buildings which lower costs. At Brighton a block of 'factory flats' has been erected.

Then there is the claim of Paul and Wyatt's modest cotton spinning mill set up in 1740 at Birmingham, powered by two donkeys and employing ten women. It was a financial failure, and was purchased by one Edward Cave (1742) and re-erected on a larger scale at Northampton. It lasted until 1764, when it was purchased by the true 'father of the factory system', Richard Arkwright. Since the factory system was born in the cotton textile industry, this particular factory could be considered the ancestor of all that followed; in the words of the doyen of industrial historians, Paul Mantoux, it was the ancestor of 'all those factories whose innumerable chimneys now (1927) surround Manchester and Glasgow, Rouen, Lowell and Chemnitz, as well as Bombay and Osaka.'

Mantoux's global assortment of examples reminds us of another revolutionary aspect of industrialism: the way in which it wears away the differences between various races and societies. Factories and coal-mines look similar anywhere in the world. Agrarian societies on the other hand had idiosyncratic architectural styles: baroque churches; pagodas; the ornate pyramids of Yucatan and the plainer ones of Egypt. To Sir Winston Churchill, who had been to South Africa in the Boer War (1899–1902), Johannesburg, from a distance, reminded him of Oldham, a Lancashire cotton town. The steel centres of Middlesbrough, Sheffield, Pittsburgh and Liège had a distinct 'family resemblance'. Not only the landscape, but societies and habits have begun to conform—a major achievement of factory-based civilisation.

The claim of Paul and Wyatt's factory is a tenuous one. A more substantial claim could be made for an establishment built in 1771 at Cromford, Derbyshire, on the banks of the River Derwent, the same river which flowed by and powered the Lombes' factory on which, indeed, the architecture of the Cromford establishment was based. This factory was the spinning mill of Richard Arkwright, and it was the very vanguard of the 'new wave' of industrialism. Whereas the Lombes', and Paul and Wyatt's had been isolated enterprises, Arkwright's mill

9

was the first of a movement which erected factories in millions all over the world and has provided the economic basis of civilisation ever since.

Why the Factory System Started

Some historians have explained the Industrial Revolution as the result of a single cause. In his classic lectures on the subject, Arnold Toynbee (1884) put it down to enlightened government policy: a more permissive attitude by the state towards business men. Others (e.g. J. R. Hicks, 1939) felt it was because of the 'population explosion'.

Common sense and investigation suggest that so mighty a change had multitudes of 'causes'. The most obvious of these can be listed.

Population Growth   The population of Great Britain began to grow quickly after about 1740 (**4**). Statistics display this clearly but why it grew is more mysterious. Suggested reasons are (i) more and better food arising out of the Agrarian Revolution (see below); (ii) earlier marriages, encouraged in turn by industrialism which offered jobs and therefore independence; (iii) better health and hygiene. This reason was once put forward as a major one, but it should be remembered that the big discoveries in medical science really date from the nineteenth century, as do the first genuine Health Laws and large hospitals. However, it is thought that the 'great pandemic' (an age in which epidemics can break out) dating from the fourteenth century was over by 1800 because by then mankind had built up resistance to certain viruses.

The birth rate remained fairly constant until modern times: it was a fall in the death rate that caused the population explosion which peopled the factory age:

Year	Birth rate (= babies born per 1,000 people)	Death rate (= people die per 1,000 people)
1751	35	30
1801	34	23
1851	33.9	22
1951	15.9	11.6

3 Exterior of an early cotton mill at Union Street, Manchester, belonging to Messrs Murray & MacConnel. It dwarfs its surroundings; a bastion of capitalism, as castles had been of feudalism in past ages.

4 It must be pointed out that not all 'urban' citizens work in factories. The proportion of factory workers decreases with the spread of automation and the growth of 'service industries' (shops, transport, clerical jobs). Thus from a peak of 32·7% of the working population in 1851, factory workers fell to 30·7% in 1881.

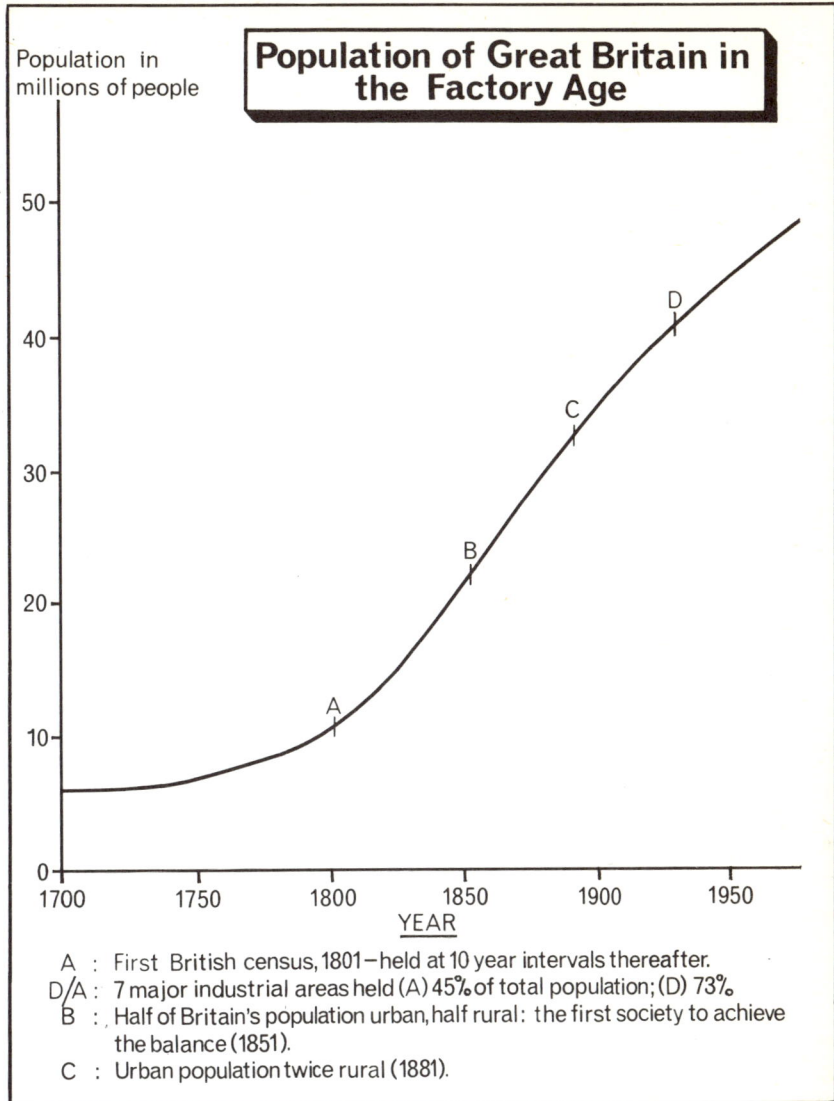

Population of Great Britain in the Factory Age

Population in millions of people

YEAR

A : First British census, 1801 – held at 10 year intervals thereafter.
D/A : 7 major industrial areas held (A) 45% of total population; (D) 73%
B : Half of Britain's population urban, half rural: the first society to achieve the balance (1851).
C : Urban population twice rural (1881).

The Agrarian (or 'Agricultural') Revolution   In the eighteenth century agriculture was made much more efficient and therefore able to feed more people. Furthermore, it achieved this with less labour per acre than before. Both of these facts were vital to creating a factory system. This change was effected by breaking up the picturesque but inefficient 'strip fields' dating from the Middle Ages, and laying out the patchwork of fields still familiar today. Some common land, often poorly used and unkempt heathland, was 'enclosed' (as the euphemism was) as well. In the Highlands of Scotland, a little later, the ex-clansmen were driven off in 'clearances' and replaced by the more docile and profitable Great Cheviot sheep. Like the English enclosures, this affair generated no little bitterness and proved that the supposedly cruel profit motive is by no means the monopoly of factory owners and 'cut-throat capitalism'. Between 1760 and 1820 more than six million acres were enclosed.

At the same time great technical improvements were introduced, e.g. seed-drilling, fattening livestock during the winter. In a sense the landowners were investing capital in land and increasing its productivity: a process which was the cousin of the industrial factory system. The traveller and writer, William Cobbett, thought that the movement had gone so far (1832) that farms he saw in the Lothians were mere 'factories for making meat and corn'.

The Commercial Revolution In order to justify factories and the expense of building them, there must be ample markets ready to absorb their products. In the Middle Ages Britain's trade was either internal, or with Europe. From about 1600 Britain tended to turn away from trading with Western Europe in order to trade with the Baltic, the Levant (Turkey, and North Africa), the Orient (India, East Indies and China) and the (then) colonies of the West Indies, Canada and North America. These colonies grew rapidly from pioneering settlements to fully fledged societies of great size (population 1700: 300,000; 1776: 3 million). As a market for British goods they were a major stimulant of economic growth. The first factories show this: they imported raw cotton from North America, processed it and sent it back there as finished goods. This is an excellent example of the growth of a world economic society; one of the elements of industrial and factory-based civilisation.

The Technical and Transport Revolutions The various machines employed in the factories are dealt with later. The key ones were Arkwright's Water Frame and Watt's improved and rotary steam engines. It is said 'necessity is the mother of invention' and the big markets and fortunes awaiting successful inventors acted as a sharp spur. Behind these inventions lay an important change in scientific attitudes—a willingness to speculate and invent marked by the great scientific philosophers such as Sir Isaac Newton.

Factories must have not only efficient machinery to make possible the division of labour, but also guaranteed supplies of raw materials to keep the machines going and render investment in them profitable. A break in the flow of raw materials or finished products can easily disrupt a factory-based economy. Therefore the factory system waited on (and developed with) modern systems of transport. First the canals (such as the Trent and Mersey, 1777) and later railways (such as the Liverpool and Manchester, 1829) and finally the modern road network gave the factory owners, often at their own expense, the transport facilities they needed.

5 Not all industry was centred in the towns. Some, like the mill of Messrs Swainson, Birley & Co. near Preston, were situated in pleasant countryside. A wonder of its age, it had an austere elegance which brooded over its rural surroundings.

6 Factories transform the night scene: early textile mills along the River Irwell, Manchester.

The Causes Combined

Other reasons for the factory system might be offered, for instance the ample funds of London merchants and wealthy landowners made available on occasion through the perfunctory banking system, to help aspiring factory owners. But most owners, it should be noted, generated their own wealth by ploughing back profits, a means of growth which required frugal living, low taxes and quickly growing markets.

Another cause is the comparative political quiet of Britain in the later eighteenth century—at least there was no major political cataclysm like the French Revolution (1789). The factory system generated its own political problems, often violent ones, but it was born in comparative political calm.

All the causes together resulted in what the American historian, W. W. Rostow, has called the 'take-off' of the British economy (into the heights of industrialism, that is) in about 1784. The age in which the causes were born and moulded he called the 'preconditions for take-off'. The world which had created the industrial system was swept away. The rapidity of this dramatic change excited wonder at first, then doubts and finally, for many observers, despair. It was finely put by the poet and mystic William Blake:

And was Jerusalem builded here
Among these dark Satanic Mills?

13

Results of the Factory System

Earlier in this Chapter Dr Arnold maintained that factories released England from feudalism—which to his vigorous and radical mind was no 'Jerusalem'. He was to be right in the long run. However, one of his contemporaries, Lord John Manners, thought 'there never was so complete a feudal system as that of the factories'. Other men raged against the new system, e.g. Thomas Carlyle and William Cobbett. Like Manners they looked back to the 'good old days' of rural England, with its stout and upright yeomen. Thus was born the Arcadian myth: the story ran that smoking factories had spoilt a decent rural society. Men used to be governed by the natural pace of the weather and the seasons—but now they were slaves or serfs of the factory hooter, and they toiled day in, day out, in smoke and darkness. (**6**)

In modern times a long controversy has gone on among historians as to whether or not the factory system really did improve the lot of the ordinary people at the time. A balanced view suggests that a tiny improvement is measurable by 1840, purely in terms of wages and the cost of living; but that unemployment, harsh conditions, the proximity of hunger and the oppressive squalor of urban conditions were bad enough to make people feel worse off. But since 1840 material conditions have improved for the bulk of the population.

The eighteenth-century man of letters, Dr Johnson, is reputed to have said that in all change only one thing is certain—the loss. By abandoning an agri-culture-based way of life and adopting a factory-based one, there have been losses. But many of the losses are welcome: inefficient agriculture and the threat of famine; gross economic and political inequality. We have gained more than mere 'Satanic Mills'—most families have more to spend and more to spend it on, because of the factory system which enables labour to become highly efficient. In the 1870s a working-class family spent three-quarters of its income on food: today the proportion is a quarter. The rest may be spent on clothes, lighting, heating and luxuries—all of which are now produced by factory methods.

As noted earlier, it tends to be a fruitless debate when someone asks: 'are we any happier now?' Unless one can commandeer some sort of time-machine as envisaged by H. G. Wells it is impossible to make comparisons. Two things may, perhaps, be said in conclusion. If a secure material welfare is necessary for human contentment, the factory system has at least made this a possibility; and, however much it may be regretted, the factory system has become the foundation of all modern economies. This book attempts to show how and why this happened, and ends by hazarding a few guesses about the future.

2 The First Factories

To many people the early history of the factory system and the rise of the cotton textile industry are virtually synonomous. This impression is erroneous, but understandable. By 1840 the majority of factories were cotton mills, yet the factory system had also been applied to pottery manufacture, iron founding and coal mining, to name a few. However, the spinning and weaving mills of the North-West were the system's most triumphant achievement. 'By the 1840s the battle had been decided in favour of the new industrial system in the theatre of textiles.' (Court.)

Textiles led the way because the requisite conditions for adopting a factory method of production were there more abundantly than in any other industry: large and expanding markets; machinery able to mass-produce; ample supplies of raw materials (imported through Liverpool); a sufficient labour force and a source of power to drive machinery in the rivers and streams running off the Pennines.

The essential key which sprung the system into action was the invention of machinery which made possible the division of labour, and so, large-scale production.

The cotton industry—the first to be extensively 'factoryised'—was, and is, not the only textile industry. Oldest of the textile trades was wool manufacture, England's 'staple industry' in the Middle Ages. It was largely based on domestic production, although fulling mills, and even giant workshops, had existed from time to time. The term 'textiles' also covers silk and linen. Cotton led the way with factory production in the eighteenth century, but its actual production was carried on by pre-industrial methods just like those of any other textile at one time. Lewes Roberts in his *Treasure of Traffike* (1641) wrote of the economy of Manchester: 'They buy Cotten wooll in London that comes first from Cyprus and Smyrna, and at home work the same, and perfit it into Fustians . . . and other such Stuffes; and then return it to London. . . .'

This early cotton industry was tiny and inferior. Anyone requiring good cotton material would import the excellent products of the East, particularly India. So great was the fashion for wearing clothes made of cotton that Parliament decreed (1700) that any further importation of printed (i.e. patterned and coloured) cotton textiles was illegal—a move designed to protect the wool industry. Enterprising businessmen found a way round this; they imported white cotton cloth and printed it in Great Britain! More clamour from the wool industry stopped this stratagem (Cotton Act 1721). Thereafter the public had to be content with wearing either plain white cotton goods (better known as calicoes or muslins) or a mixture of cotton and linen (legalised in 1736)—or woollens.

However, developments elsewhere were acting in the interests of the cotton industry. Political chaos in India destroyed the main supplier of cotton textiles: a rich reward awaited India's successor. New supplies of raw cotton were entering the growing world trading system from Brazil and the West Indies, and, rather later the 'South' of what was to become the U.S.A. The supplies of raw cotton to Europe tended to be funnelled through Liverpool, a port on the western seaboard, marginally nearer the new sources.

The cotton industry was labouring under the hostile laws mentioned above (not repealed until 1774) and clumsy methods of production. These were embodied in the domestic system, whereby a mass of cottage workers (or 'outworkers'), often part-time small farmers, received raw cotton from a 'master' who undertook to purchase finished goods from the workers. These he duly sold at a profit to himself. The domestic workers had to card (remove knots), spin and weave the cotton; the complete antithesis of the intensive division of labour which was to come. Broadly speaking, the factory system was the process by which some masters built a special establishment where either spinning, or weaving, went on: not both. They employed a permanent force of labour; the individual labourer became a worker and nothing else—least of all a part-time farmer. So was born the industrial working class.

The transition from domestic to factory production was marked by the introduction of special machinery. In 1733 *Kay's Flying Shuttle* made weaving more efficient, but it was convenient enough to be used domestically, not requiring special buildings to house it. By speeding up the weaving process it created a big demand for cotton yarn with which to do the weaving. A number of men applied themselves to producing a spinning machine which would answer this need. The first known was *Wyatt's Spinning Machine* (1733) which, it was claimed by his son, 'spun the first thread of cotton ever produced without the intervention of human

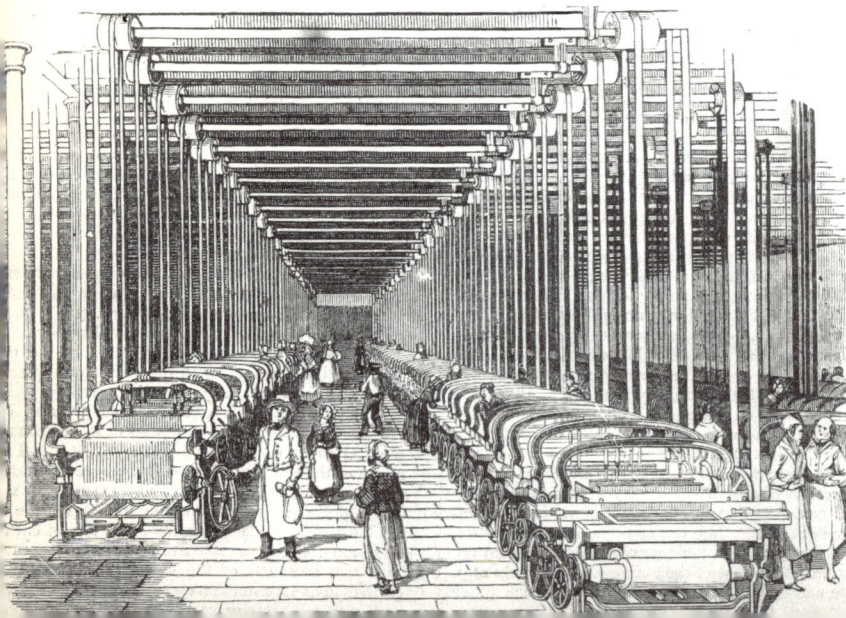

7 Power looms in an early cotton mill. A steam engine (unseen) drives the overhead shafts, connected by belts to the looms. The picture hints at the grand scale and intense monotony of such factories.

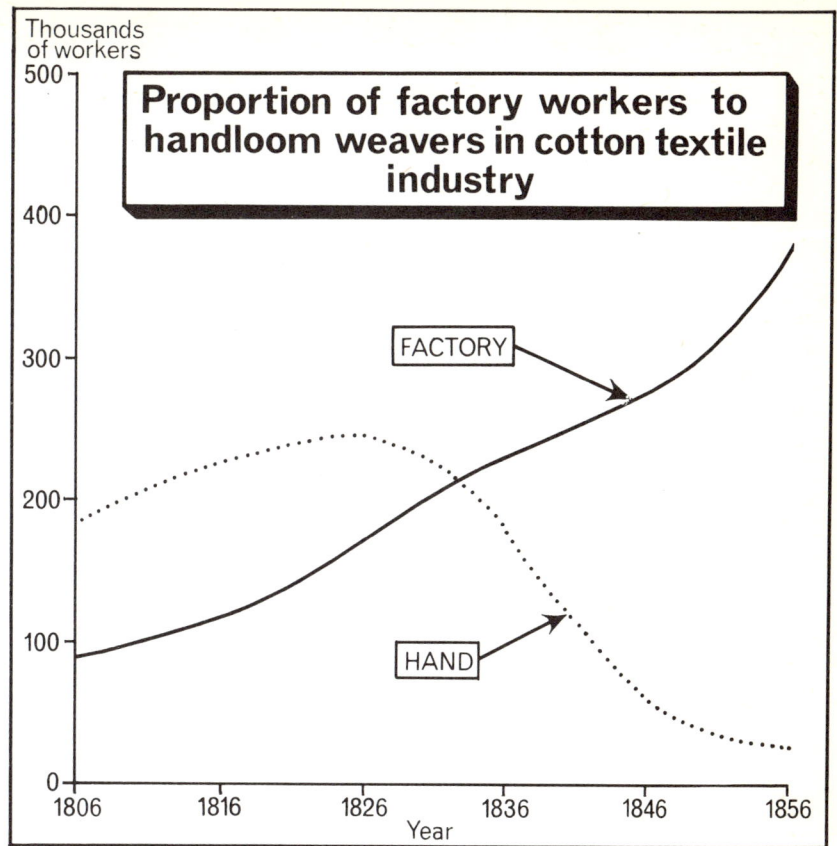

Proportion of factory workers to handloom weavers in cotton textile industry

Thousands of workers

FACTORY

HAND

fingers'. The factory of Wyatt and his partner, Paul (p. 9) was a failure, and his machine which he called a 'gymcrack of some consequence' was (after its sale to Cave) eventually lost without trace.

Wyatt's successors and their machines have been more accurately recorded; indeed they almost rank with '1066' as universally familiar history. They were:
1. *Hargreaves' Spinning Jenny* (c. 1767), which enabled one man to work, in effect, eight spinning machines at once. Like Kay's apparatus it was not necessarily large and could be erected by a domestic spinner.
2. *Arkwright's Water Frame* (1769), so called because its large size required water power to work it. It was this machine, therefore, which demanded special buildings and really laid the foundation of the cotton factory system.
3. *Crompton's Mule* (1776) which combined the ideas of Hargreaves and Arkwright (hence its name: a hard-working cross-breed) and made it possible to produce yarn at once fine (like the Jenny's) and tough (like the Water Frame's). The mule could be used domestically or in a factory. The great advantage of the factory system was, thanks to Arkwright's enterprise, readily apparent by Crompton's time and many really large mules were erected in factory buildings.
4. So far the inventions referred to have been spinning machines. The quantities of yarn being produced by the 1780s created a shortage of weaving establishments able to absorb and use yarn. The hand-loom weavers were enjoying an Indian Summer of opulence, and some were said to strut about with £5 notes (worth over £50 today) stuck ostentatiously in their hats. Their prosperity came from the

Mechanisation: a dramatic change effected by machinery: **9** *(left)* shows the laborious hand printing of calico (1754); **10** *(right)* shows mechanical rotary printing (1834) which was quicker and more accurate. The expensive machinery was justified by the big markets awaiting printed cotton cloth which was a true child of the factory age, like the other cotton textile trades.

weaving bottleneck. How to weave quickly and cheaply? The answer was *Cartwright's Loom* (1785) which made mass-produced woven goods possible and spelt doom for the hand-loom weavers. For instance, the prices for weaving muslins at Bolton, Lancs., fell from 3s. per yard (1792) to 1s. 2d. per yard (1799). The power loom could be activated by water or steam, although one early example (Robertson of Glasgow, 1793) employed dog-power!

5. Some other textile machinery inventions of importance were the Ring Spinning Frame (an improved mule; 1830); cotton combing machines (1847); and roller printing (**10**). All these machines removed various bottlenecks and mechanised yet another part of the production flow from raw cotton to finished (or 'piece') goods.

Water-powered mills tended to be erratic because the flow of rivers is not constant, but varies seasonally. Some mills built reservoirs to even out the flow and Arkwright's factory at Cromford, Derbyshire, was driven by a river fed by a warm spring—which conveniently kept production going even in hard winters. Early steam engines were a better solution to the problem of constant power. The first true steam-powered mills were Robinson's spinning mill at Papplewick (1785) and, in weaving, John Monteith's mill (1800).

But it must not be supposed that either the factory system or machinery were adopted in an excited rush. On the contrary, the change was slow. By 1833 half of the powered mills were still operated by water. Early steam engines were expensive and unreliable; the cost of investing in a specially built factory was very great and it was often cheaper to continue with the 'putting-out system' (the combination of travelling masters and cottage workers). The domestic workers clung to their way of life, often in the depths of poverty, because at least they felt 'free'

and were loath to surrender to the toil and discipline of a mill owned by somebody else.

Yet the system of factories and the division of labour arrived gradually and inexorably (**8**). As markets expanded, machines became more reliable and bulk supplies of raw cotton were plentiful and cheap. The pressure to abandon 'putting out' and to invest in factories increasingly tempted the masters. The economic reasons were compelling: the costs, fancied and real, to civilisation appear in Chapter 4.

The First Mills

Most of the inventors noted above failed to exploit their ideas successfully. Cartwright was a clergyman with a clever but butterfly brain; a poet, classicist and experimenter—emphatically not an astute man of business. Arkwright 'heralded the new age' in many ways, not merely because of his machinery and factories, but because of his excellent business brain, a mixture of caution, speed, speculation and toughness. He looked for, and found, equally shrewd backers to supply him with the money required to start factory production on some scale. Aided by them, Arkwright erected his mills, really the first of modern times, at Cromford (1771); Belper (1776); and Manchester (1780).

These mills were in the Derbyshire–Lancashire–Cheshire area, a location dictated by the proximity of Pennine water power and the port of Liverpool. By coincidence the damp climate of the area made spinning easier (thread is less likely to snap in a humid atmosphere). The climate was not a governing factor, although a persistent legend claims it was, as if Arkwright had tramped England with an hygrometer. Similar conditions held in Lanarkshire, Scotland, where other early textile mills were built.

Near to the spinning and weaving mills various finishing processes went on; such as bleaching (making the cloth white); or dyeing and printing. To keep pace with factory production these processes had to be mechanised as well (**9**) (**10**). By 1830 the factory system was clearly established in the cotton textile industry. It employed 450,000 workers and as such was the biggest industrial employer of labour in Great Britain. There were seven big mills which employed over 1000 people; 23 employed over 500 and another 36 over 250. Arkwright's son employed 2,000 spinners at Cromford, and at New Lanark Messrs Owen and Dale employed 1,600. Besides these giants there were many small masters owning factories which were supplying the world with cotton goods, or as they significantly became known: 'Manchester Goods': Grant Bros. of Ramsbottom; Greg & Sons of Manchester; and the seven Ashton brothers of Hyde.

Thomas Carlyle sensed the destiny in Richard Arkwright, who had risen from village barber to industrial tycoon: 'O reader, what a historical phenomenon is that bag-cheeked, pot-bellied, much enduring, much inventing barber!'

Factories and Wool

A government report of 1840 produced the following table of comparative statistics relating to power looms as at 1835:

	Cotton	Wool	Silk	Flax	Mixed	Total
England:	96,679	5,105	1,714	41	25	103,564
Scotland:	17,531	22	—	168	—	17,721

Clearly the ancient wool industry had fallen behind in the adoption of machinery and factories. This was in spite of its selfish demands for protective laws in the early eighteenth century. The slowness with which the factory system developed in this case is not difficult to understand.

First, wool fibres were much more difficult to work by machinery than cotton fibres. Second, cotton was a comparatively new and adventurous industry, willing by its nature to try new ideas; wool was long established and suffering from 'inertia'. Full of confidence and ancient traditions, it relied on domestic production and fairly small-scale methods, although bulk buying of raw wool at large fairs (e.g. Stourbridge) and large-scale marketing at the 'piece halls' of Leeds and Halifax were well established. Still, these were methods of marketing, not production. The third reason was that a factory system needed a copious and guaranteed supply of raw materials to justify the high cost of factory buildings. This was not forthcoming in the wool industry until Australia began to supply bulk quantities of wool in the 1830s. The modest home 'clip' certainly did not provide a reliable basis for factory methods.

11 Titus Salt's masterpiece: the factory and model town of Saltaire (near Bradford, Yorkshire) dating from 1853. Seen here in 1896, this giant factory was served by rail, river and canal to bring raw materials and take away finished products. In its early years it contained two miles of shafting (weighing 700 tons) and could make 5,600 miles of alpaca cloth a year 'which, as the crow flies, would almost reach the native mountains of the alpaca'—(Mr Fairbairn, its engineer-designer).

The newer trade in worsteds was first off the mark with machine spinning; the first powered worsted mill was at Addingham (near Skipton, Yorkshire), 1787. The 'father' of the factory system in the wool trade was Benjamin Gott of Leeds who set up two large factories and by 1800 employed steam power in them. By the 1830s factory spinning for worsted was well established. While Yorkshire adopted the factory system, its old rivals in the wool textile industry, East Anglia and the West Country, did not. By the 1840s, with a few exceptions, their woollen industries had perished.

Whereas the cotton hand-loom weavers were almost expunged by the 1860s, hand-loom weavers still produced half the woollen cloth at that time. Hand-combing of raw wool was the rule until the 1840s, when Cunliffe-Lister's wool combing machine removed the 'most intransigent and persistent bottleneck in the handling of wool' (Checkland). It allowed one man to do the work of 100 skilled hand-combers, and to do it far better. This is another striking example of capital (the machine) raising the productivity of labour; of the superiority in quantity and quality of factory production over domestic production and of the mechanisation of one process pushing other component processes into factory methods, like breaking a log-jam in a river.

21

The Potteries

Another industry which adopted factory methods earlier than most was the pottery industry. During the Industrial Revolution, first earthenware (covered with a thin glaze) and later china, or 'porcelain' (glazed throughout), became mass-produced. As in the case of cotton textiles, technical improvements were discovered which encouraged large-scale production. The growing markets which justified such methods were being touched by Britain's increasing commerce and cultivated by the aggressive salesmanship of the master potters.

Improved ways of shaping pottery were adopted after about 1730, when moulding replaced the potter's wheel for all but the most artistic work. Better methods of glazing were introduced: salt glazing and lead glazing, and a pleasant white colour was produced by including some crushed flint in the clay. The human cost of these innovations was very considerable (p. 75) but, technically, the 'Potteries' of North Staffordshire were easily ahead of the world by the 1780s.

A large market is, as we have seen, essential for the factory system. Greatest of the master potters at finding and satisfying new markets was Josiah Wedgwood (1730–95). He was strictly 'consumer oriented' as modern business jargon has it: he paced his potteries looking for defective products which might lose him custom. If found, they were instantly smashed and the irate master would chalk on the erring potter's bench: 'This won't do for Josiah Wedgwood'—an early form of what is today called 'quality control'. He developed new and popular lines of ware green glaze, creamware and black basalt—which are now collectors' items. He believed in the division of labour, and in rigorous training for his specialist employees, wanting, as he said, to 'make such machines of the men as they cannot err'.

His particular *métier* was marketing. He was quick to sense the slightest change in fashion or demand. This was the era when tea drinking first became widespread in Britain, so Wedgwood produced tea-sets. Classical taste became the rage, so Wedgwood produced imitation Etruscan vases (he even called his factory 'Etruria'). He set up showrooms in London, Bath and Liverpool, used newspaper advertising and employed travelling salesmen. He could indeed boast that he was 'vase-maker general to the Universe'.

By the 1770s, therefore, the potteries had technical improvements, ample raw materials and big markets. One barrier remained: distance. The transport of china clay was restricted by the slow and expensive mule-trains. Returning to Liverpool, or London with finished goods, the rough journeying resulted in a high proportion of breakages. Wedgwood and others could not tolerate such conditions and duly built themselves a canal (Trent and Mersey Canal, 1777) so that smooth waterways could carry both raw materials to Staffordshire, and the finished products away.

Wedgwood had many rivals, such as the Spode family, one of whom (Josiah Spode) concentrated on the mass market awaiting cheap china.

Mechanical power was adopted slowly in the pottery industry; it is recorded

12 Longton, near Stoke-on-Trent (Arnold Bennett's 'Longshaw') firing its bottle kilns about 1900. Soon St James's church *(left)* and all else will be obscured in a universal fog. Modern firing methods have released the Potteries from this noxious industrial blanket.

that a steam engine was used as early as 1793 to drive flint crushing machinery, but even as late as 1845 'the whole range of mechanical science was almost solely represented in the manufacture of potting by the thrower's wheel— identical in mechanical principle . . . with that used by the ancient Egyptians'. (Owen).

Nevertheless, by 1830 the big potteries had capitalistic production and sup-plied big markets. By 1836 the Trent and Mersey Canal was taking away 73,500 tons of earthenware and china annually, and it brought in 70,000 tons of clay and 30,000 tons of flint. By 1843 the eighty main pottery employers had 12,400 men working for them: by the standards of the day, this was a big industry.

The industry generated more atmospheric filth and pollution than almost any other. Before the advent of electrical firing a grim industrial joke at the expense of the pottery city, Stoke-on-Trent, was the all-black postcard picture simply entitled: 'When Stoke stokes'. The spread of the factory system in other industries was to be accompanied by a similar and tragic price.

23

Coal, Iron and Metals

Like pottery and cotton, mining and metalworking are industries which antedate the factory system, but were to be early and spectacular beneficiaries of it. The growth of coal mining in Great Britain during the Industrial Revolution was swift:

Year	Output in tons	Year	Output in tons
1700	2,148,000	1790	7,618,728
1750	4,773,828	1795	10,080,300
1770	6,205,400	1854	64,700,000

Two elements lay behind this growth—the technical improvements rendering large-scale and deep mining possible, and the growing demand for coal from domestic users for heating, from iron works for smelting and from steam powered factories (and later railways) for fuel. As with all examples of industrial growth, many factors were inter-connected: the building of railways required iron; railways used coal and made it possible to move it cheaply and in bulk to the new cities of the industrial age; as a result coal mining prospered.

13 *(left)* A primitive coal mine in the pre-industrial age: winding wheels were then worked by horse-power. 14 *(right)* Jarrow colliery (*c.* 1840) in the early mechanical (or 'palaeotechnic') age. It had two steam winding engines of 80 *h.p.* and 43 *h.p.* respectively and a 90 *h.p.* pumping engine. Mechanisation enabled deeper working (175 fathoms = 1,050 feet), but led to more accidents. Between 1820 and 1830 nearly 100 pitmen were killed here—42 at once in an explosion in August, 1830. This pit was connected to the River Tyne by an inclined plane. At the time shown it produced 28,700 tons a year.

15 St Helen's Colliery, near Workington, Cumberland, *c.* 1924. This mill was fully mechanised at the surface and was served by rail—both factors encouraging large-scale output. It produced over 150,000 tons a year before its closure (1966). Opened in 1877, it was owned by the St Helen's Colliery & Brickworks Co. Ltd and was nationalised with the bulk of the coal industry in 1946.

The technical improvements were:

1. A series of improved steam engines, which pumped mines free of water and so allowed deeper seams to be tapped. They were the comparatively crude Savery engine (1698) and Newcomen engine (1705); and the efficient engine of James Watt (1769). Of various types there were roughly 60 at work in the 1720s (13 of these in the North-East coalfield) and over 1,300 by 1800, a heavy concentration of which were also at work in various pits between the Rivers Tyne and Wear. The lead mines of Derby and the copper mines of Cornwall were also big users of steam pumping engines.

Steam engines were used elsewhere, e.g. in cotton mills and even by a Mr Joseph Fry of Bristol, a chocolate manufacturer (1797). Generally, however, the early engines were crude and expensive and not very flexible in operation, qualities which restricted their employment.

2. Miscellaneous developments which increased production were the safety lamp (1815) which provided underground illumination with relative safety; the strong wire rope (1839) for hauling coal to the surface; and the exhaust fan (1837) for ventilating the stifling lower depths of the mines (**13**, **14**, **15**).

16 The large amount of capital invested in the mechanisation of mining is shown in this intriguing underground photograph of what is believed to be Grenville United Mines, near Camborne, Cornwall. This is the massive pumping apparatus necessary to prevent flooding.

Iron   The connexion between iron and coal was manifest in many ways. Coal, converted into coke, was increasingly used from 1750 onwards to smelt (turn ore into metal) the iron. The industry moved from its traditional home, Sussex, where charcoal from the denuded oak forests had been used for smelting, to the Severn Valley, South Wales and Central Scotland where iron and coal were found close together. Sussex was an early example of regional industrial decline: there was only one furnace left there by 1796 (at Ashburnham) and this closed in 1828 (**17**). Coal mines needed steam engines, and these were made of iron. Two men were able to work iron exactly enough to produce a viable engine: Matthew Boulton, partner of James Watt and owner of the famous light engineering factory at Soho (**19**), who produced the main components of Watt's engine; and John Wilkinson, an ironmaster, who bored the cylinders. In turn, Wilkinson was one of Boulton and Watt's first customers, using a steam engine to work the giant bellows at Coalbrookdale (**18**) which blasted air into the iron furnaces.

17 *The Iron Forge* by Joseph Wright of Derby (1779) shows ironworking in the pre-factory era. The 'trip hammer', actuated by a water-driven drum, beats red-hot iron. The inclusion of the ironworker's family emphasises the domestic nature of the industry.

Coalbrookdale has been called the 'cradle of the Industrial Revolution'—for here heavy, or basic industry, employing factory methods began. But, for all its technical progress, Coalbrookdale did not introduce such a growth as Ark-wright's mills. Nevertheless, the ironworks there were rated one of the main sights of the time, giving some warning that they were the ancestor of the great steel cities of the future. Arthur Young wrote of them (1776): 'A winding glen between immense hills . . . all thickly covered in wood . . . too beautiful to be in unison with the variety of horrors art has spread at the bottom; the noise of the forges, mills, etc., with all their vast machinery, the flame bursting from the furnaces with the burning of the coal and the smoak of the limekilns. . . .'

Blasting engines were only one technical innovation in the iron industry. Other important ones were:

1. *Coke* first used in place of charcoal, by Abraham Darby, *c.* 1709.
2. *Sand* used for moulding molten metal into 'pigs', *c.* 1707.

27

18 de Loutherbourg's aquatint of Wilkinson's mechanised iron works at Coalbrookdale. Note iron pipes lying about, and the rural background remarked on by Arthur Young (p. 27).

3. *'Puddling'*—a purifying process; and the rolling of hot metal over steam engine driven rollers (hence the term 'rolling mills') by Henry Cort, 1784.

4. The *'Hot Blast'* which saves fuel, by Neilson, 1828.

These innovations removed the iron industry from its romantic and rural setting in the Weald, dotted with tiny charcoal furnaces and turf huts, to the large and expensive complexes of works in the Black Country (**54**), South Wales, etc. These newer and larger works, served by advanced machinery, allowed the division of labour on a big scale: they contained blast furnaces, rolling mills, engine houses and kilns. Although these processes were not carried on literally under one roof, this was essentially factory production.

19 Boulton's 'manufactory' at Soho, near Birmingham. The customers were affluent 'carriage trade', not yet a mass market.

20, 21 and **22** show the three stages in the history of cutlery manufacture. **20** shows the slow hand-production of razors in a workshop, *c. 1815.*

The finished metal was often worked elsewhere, for instance in the workshops of Sheffield (**21**) or Birmingham, where myriads of varieties of ironware (pins, nails, axes, knives, etc.)—called 'toys' in the trade—were produced. Boulton's Soho factory concentrated many of these processes in one building. Work there was carefully subdivided so that certain workmen produced certain goods, and so developed special skills and worked more efficiently. This was the division of labour of an early and obvious kind. It was not entirely by coincidence that Adam Smith, the first major economist of modern times, used the example of a pin factory to illustrate the division of labour in his great work, *The Wealth of Nations* (1776).

The iron industry developed so quickly that by 1800 it led Europe and indeed the world, having been an 'also ran' for centuries. In 1700 Britain imported two-thirds of its iron needs from Sweden and Russia. By 1830 it was exporting more than it imported (technically referred to as a *net exporter*).

Year	Output of pig iron	Imports		Exports	
1700	not known	17,000	England	2,000	
1720	25,000	23,600	and	1,900	
1788	68,300	51,400	Wales	13,700	
1806	243,851	33,000		28,000	
1830	677,417	14,900	G.B.	118,000	including
1840	1,396,400	5,700		269,000	steel

Although not so powerful as cotton textiles, the iron industry was nevertheless the new capitalism on the grand scale. In 1812 ten ironworks, each costing

21 The arrival of mechanisation brings (1866) mechanical grinding of razors in Sheffield. The industry, however, was still labour intensive. Note the spare grinding wheels stacked in the roof.

£50,000, were erected near Birmingham alone. The demand generated by the war with France (1792–1815) acted as a forcing house for the industry and great ironworks seemed to sprout up and enchant the intelligent traveller, such as the Swede, Erik Svedenstjerna (1802), who wrote of the South Wales iron town, Merthyr Tydfil: 'some 20 years ago it was but an insignificant village, but the works now established there have . . . made it one of the most interesting places in the whole kingdom'. He saw there in a single half mile (Swedish) 13 blast furnaces and 25 puddling furnaces, a 52-foot water wheel, numerous 70- and 80-h.p. steam engines and vast coal mines owned by the ironmasters, social giants of the day such as Guest of Dowlais, Crawshay of Cyfarthfa who left £1½ millions, and Homfray of Pen-y-Darran, the employer of 4,000 men.

Svedenstjerna's contemporary, the French geologist, de Saint-Ford, went to the Carron ironworks in Scotland (1784) where he was intrigued by 'huge cranes, every kind of windlass . . . the creaking, the piercing noise of the pulleys, the continuous sound of hammering, the ceaseless energy of the men keeping all this machinery in motion . . .'. At night he recorded: '. . . here a glowing mass of coal, there darting flames . . . the heavy hammers striking the echoing anvils and the shrill whistle of the air pumps . . .'. He went on to wonder: '. . . whether we are looking at a volcano in eruption or have been miraculously transported to Vulcan's cave where he and his cyclops are manufacturing lightning'.

The iron was being bought at home and abroad, for 'toys', machinery and armaments, and building purposes. It was used in the revolutionary Albion Flour Mills in London (1785), the world's first factory to use all-metal plant and

30

22 The modern factory of Messrs Wilkinson Sword, at Cramlington, Northumberland, uses advanced machinery to produce millions of razor blades a week (1968).

machinery. It supplied the building framework of early cotton mills, and was attractive to the owners because it carried less fire risk than wooden beams. It was used to construct networks of tramways and railways in the coalfields, to make hundreds of miles of pipeline to carry gas and water in urban areas—John Wilkinson made 40 miles of it for Paris alone. An iron bridge was put over the Severn at Broseley, near Coalbrookdale, in 1779. John Wilkinson experimented endlessly in order to find uses for his iron: he built an iron barge in 1787, and was suitably buried in an iron coffin (1805). (**23**) (**24**)

Metal Mining and Refining

The growth of the iron industry should not be allowed to obscure the spectacular progress of mineral mining at the time. Here, as with coal and iron, capital was being applied to the mines to mechanise them and render them more productive.

The richest area of such enterprise was Cornwall, for many years the world's leading producer of copper ore. The shallow mines were restricted by primitive technology, e.g. the use of horse-driven 'whims' which hauled wooden cages to the surface. By 1740 Cornwall mined more copper (11,007 tons) than the 'staple' metal of the country, tin, in spite of the crude methods employed. What really released the industry and lifted it into the new industrial era was the application of the steam engine which enabled the mines to be worked to a much greater depth and tap rich reserves of ore. (**16**)

23 and **24** show the different ways in which artists treated industrial subjects, in this instance, ironworks. **23** The artist, T. Allom, emphasises the romantic and exciting aspects of Lymington ironworks, near Newcastle Upon Tyne (1835).

Cornwall was one of Boulton and Watt's best markets for steam engines: 40 engines were installed there between 1770 and 1780 alone. It produced some of the master-engineers of steam, notably Trevithick and Woolf. Because Cornwall had no coal it had to come by sea; great emphasis was therefore placed on raising the efficiency of engines in Cornwall. These engines, easier on fuel than many contemporaries, were housed in rugged engine houses which were once a characteristic part of the Cornish scene (**25**). The Cornish engine was in demand, 'known throughout the world, famous alike for its simplicity, economy and efficiency' (Barton). Once again, inter-relating factors spurred industrial growth.

By 1838 Cornwall was producing 147,000 tons of copper ore in such delightfully named mines as Tresavean, Wheal Jewel and North Roskear. At Tresavean another interesting innovation was employed (1843)—the 'man engine', a form of mechanical ladder which enabled miners to reach workings at a depth of 1,680 feet in 25 minutes. Previously the journey had taken an exhausting hour: a clear and excellent example of capital being employed to increase the productivity of labour.

The copper and tin ores of Cornwall were sent to South Wales for refining into pure copper and tin.

Tinplate   The tinplate industry had been centred in Germany for centuries and was introduced into Great Britain by Major John Hanbury of Pontypool, Wales, in the early eighteenth century, and shortly afterwards into England by an observer of the Welsh works who recorded in his account: 'paid for information in tinning, £36 15s. od.'—an early example of industrial espionage. The difficult tinning process involved coating very thin sheets of iron with molten tin; this tinplate was then sold to a tinsmith who fashioned it into lamps, pans, containers, etc.

A typical early mill (at Melingriffith, near Cardiff) was producing (by 1771) 4,200 boxes of tin (one 'box' = 112 sheets) and 18,000 by 1800. Great Britain as a whole produced 14,000 tons of tinplate at the beginning of the nineteenth century, and over half a million tons at the end. The growth of the industry was aided by heavy capital investment, such as steam-driven mills and mechanically

24 shows the prosaic and descriptive style of *Steam Engine Manufactory and Iron-Works, Bolton* by Harwood (1829). Boilers, tubes and engine beams can be seen in the well-integrated plant of Messrs Rothwell, Hick & Co.

operated tinning pots. This mechanisation raised the productivity of labour:

1860 a 12-hour shift produced 30 tons of tinplate.

1880 an 8-hour shift produced 36 tons of tinplate.

As in other cases, factory methods required large sources of raw materials (Cornwall and overseas) and expanding markets. Packing cases, kitchen utensils and tin cans for food (p. 48) were all in large and growing demand throughout the nineteenth century.

In the early tinplate 'works' one found the division of labour which marks factory methods: the forge which prepared the iron to be covered; the 'black plate mill' which rolled the iron into thin sheets and the tinning house where the final coating took place. The industry stimulated others: for instance, it needed certain acids and so created a demand for heavy chemicals. The traveller, Svedenstjerna, noted activity around the metal working capital, Swansea: '. . . such a number of copper works, coal mines, water tanks, canals, aqueducts and railroads can be seen crowded together, that a new visitor will hardly know to which object he should first give his attention.'

The smaller metalworking industries summarise the state of factory production

25 At Wheal Grenville, Cornwall, *c.* 1890, mechanical 'stamps' crushed the ore with greater speed and efficiency than hand labour could ever achieve—also with greater noise. The clatter of this machinery was legendary.

26 Food factories: a mid-nineteenth-century panorama of the sugar refining centre of Greenock, Renfrewshire, whose first refinery dates from 1765. Raw materials arrived in bulk by sea. Greenock's early adoption of advanced processes (e.g. vacuum boiling and centrifugal drying) gave it the lead in sugar refining and earned it the heavy nickname of *Saccharopolis*: the 'city of sugar'. The smoking chimney on the right belongs to Messrs Neil, Dempster & Neil, refiners.

in the early nineteenth century. It was novel and exciting to curious minds of the time; it demonstrated that production could expand and the efficiency of labour rise if capital was employed in the form of special buildings, machines, processes and improved communications. The mills of Lancashire, the engine houses of Cornwall and the blazing ironworks of the Black Country were the harbingers of the new civilisation.

Reading List
T. S. Ashton: *The Industrial Revolution*
D. B. Barton: *Historic Cornish Mining Scenes Underground*
　　　,,　　　*A History of Tin Mining and Smelting in Cornwall*
W. H. B. Court: *A Concise Economic History of Britain 1750–Recent Times*
R. H. Campbell: *Carron Company*
L. T. C. Rolt: *James Watt*
S. D. Chapman: *The Early Factory Masters*
Jennifer Tann: *Gloucestershire Woollen Mills*

3 The Factory System Triumphant, 1840–1914

From the 1840s to the First World War (1914–18) the factory system made many conquests. It captured old industries (such as boot- and shoe-making) and dominated many new ones from birth, such as industrial chemicals and electric power generation. This achievement was the work of the privately-owned industrial system loosely known as 'capitalism', as opposed to state-owned industry usually referred to as 'socialism'.

The Victorian age was the golden age of capitalism, whose achievements seemed, by 1900, to be gigantic and illimitable. However, in spite of the power of the system—with its Forth Bridge; ocean liners; thousands of miles of railways and millions of acres of smoking factory-cities—there were some important gaps which had to be filled by the state: education, care for the old and unemployed, in addition to the traditional state functions of maintaining law and order and defending society with armed forces.

In time the state nationalised (i.e. purchased compulsorily) various industries and is now (1969) the proprietor of coal mines, gas works, power stations and steel mills. This compromise between private and state ownership is called a 'mixed economy'. However, such a development was hardly imagined before the Great War and the victory of the factory system came about under the aegis of capitalism.

Because the spread of factories brought much suffering, capitalism was, by inference, blamed. By the turn of the century it had many enemies: socialists, communists, syndicalists, etc., all of whom offered remedies to the problem and their own formulas for a new society. However, on the occasions when capitalism has been replaced, the factories and their methods have remained. There is no other means known of producing the goods required by modern societies: it is the framework of ownership, not the methods of production, which have changed.

Textiles

Cotton textiles, the classic factory product of the Industrial Revolution, were being produced overwhelmingly in factories by 1840. In the next 80 years the industry became, together with coal, iron and steel, one of the 'old staple' industries of modern times—a pillar of the economy. Also, during the same period, other textile industries, whose factory development had been slow to 1840, became completely mechanised and their production was housed in factories. Not only were there

27 Mechanical engineering: many British railways made their own rolling stock. Here at Crewe (1913) a London and North Western Railway engine is being lifted in the erecting shop. Opened in 1843, this works was making 50,000 tons of steel a year by 1913, rolling much of it into the L.N.W.R.'s rails; building about 100 engines a year and employing 7,600 men. Some private firms built engines for home and overseas—a valuable source of foreign exchange in the steam age.

more textile factories, but the size of the average factory grew, as larger markets and abundant raw materials justified the change:

Textile	Average employees in mill	
	1838	1870
Cotton	137	177
Wool	46	70
Worsted	76	175

In 1844 the average worker in a spinning mill produced 2,800 lb. of yarn; in 1880 he (or more likely she) produced 5,500 lb.—a marked rise in productivity. The remaining domestic hand-spinners could not compete with the mechanised efficiency of factory spinning: they were extinct in Scotland by 1887 and in England by 1900 (a remarkable case of survival, nevertheless). In weaving the story was similar. A mere handful of hand-loom weavers held out until the 1890s. They had to face the remorseless growth of productivity in weaving mills: 1,700 lb. of cloth per worker (1844) to 4,000 lb. per worker (1880). The worsted industry had an even more complete and ruthless record: by 1855 there were no worsted hand spinners and very few hand weavers. In wool hand-loom weaving survived longer: even in 1866 it accounted for a quarter of all production, but, as noted, factory methods were adopted slowly in this industry. The factory system spread to *flax*, *hemp* and *jute* production, again at the expense of hand workers:

	Flax power looms in 1835	1885
England	41	4,000
Scotland	168	21,600
Ireland	100	22,000

A latecomer to factory methods was the *hosiery* industry which was organised, as late as 1850, on pre-factory lines. Like the cotton and wool industries before the time of Arkwright and Gott it still employed 'outworkers'. In 1860 there were only 3,500 factory workers in hosiery (mainly around Nottingham) as opposed to

28 Shipbuilding: the hand-built *Southernfield* being fashioned at R. Ritson & Co.'s yard, Maryport, Cumberland (1881). The small average size of such vessels, and the simple technology of the time, permitted workshop construction (cf. **29**).

50,000 domestic knitters. These domestic workers were not hardy independents; they hired their frame machines from 'middlemen' (i.e. masters) at high rents and made little profit. Yet this seemed to keep the hated hosiery factories at bay, although these were 'only glorified frame shops' (Clapham). It is said that the hand-knitters were given artificial encouragement to survive by the archaic and peculiar War Office specifications for army pants, which were virtually impossible to machine-knit!

The factory system waited on technical improvements, as it had done in

29 shows but one corner of the machine shop of Messrs Cammell Laird's shipyard, Birkenhead. Shipbuilding in the age of steel and engines adopted factory methods for part of the process.

Gas Works: industrial cities—and others—had factory-made heat and light, a major revolution after thousands of years of candle- and lamp-light. **30** *(left)* Oldham, Lancashire, gas works (*c.* 1880) owned by the borough and supplying 25,000 consumers via 106 miles of mains. **31** *(right)* Part of the mammoth Beckton works of the Gas Light & Coke Co., showing No. 12 horizontal

cotton textiles a hundred years before. A government inspector in the *Factory Report 1904* noted 'the new automatic knitting machine can only be driven by power'. The hosiery factories adopting it tended to be small, but were still true factories: another stronghold of traditional craftsmanship had fallen. Another minor textile industry which compromised with the factories was the lace industry. The settlement here was a hybrid: part domestic, part factory. In 1831 there were 22 power-driven lace factories, employing 3,000 workers. However, many clients preferred hand-made lace so complete mechanisation never occurred.

The textile industries enjoyed expansion and prosperity up to 1914, although flax and silk languished partly from foreign competition—a grim omen for the future. It was the great age of cotton: men called Manchester 'Cottonopolis' (the city of cotton) and boasted that no rival could challenge the mills of Lancashire. Mills grew still further in size: in 1884 the typical spinning mill housed 25,000 spindles, in 1911 some 60,000. A last fling of expansion (1905–14) answered the needs of growing overseas markets and created new and splendid mills; 95 in 1905–07 alone, housing 8,500,000 spindles. This expansion rested on a shaky foundation, and the 50 tragic years after 1918 were to show some of the disadvantages of a factory-based economy; ironically through the collapse of the first factory industry of all.

38

retort house (1932) where coal gas was generated for the London network. Specially built to receive sea-borne bulk coal (1868–70), Beckton came to cover 300 acres and contain 45 miles of railway. Both undertakings shown here were nationalised in 1948. Natural gas will release much of the industry from laborious factory generation in the future.

Steam and Iron

Because of its reliance on coal, nineteenth-century industrial society was once described as 'carboniferous capitalism' (A. E. Smailes)—steam and free enterprise. Coal was absolutely basic to that society; it helped to build and actually powered railways, factories, ships, gasworks, etc. (**27**, **28**, **29**, **30**, **31**): to an economist of 1865, Stanley Jevons, it seemed that coal 'commands this age'. Iron and steel makers were major users of coal, both employed factory methods, and the size and complexity of their capital equipment grew as the century progressed. The new iron-town of Middlesbrough, Yorkshire, exemplified the best

32 Steelworks: heavy industry's huge capital investment is shown in this picture of the Branch End Iron & Steel Works of Messrs Bolckow, Vaughan & Co. at Middlesbrough, c. 1900.

33 *The Forge*: a steel engraving (1859) by James Sharples, artist, trade unionist and foundry foreman, who etched this picture in his spare time over 10 years. Sharples spent his life on the factory floor and this record of a Blackburn iron foundry captures the spirit of the place with technical accuracy.

in British iron working (**32**), it was built with great rapidity and was praised by the statesman, Gladstone, as the 'infant Hercules of the North'. The average British blast furnace made 120 tons of iron a week in the 1840s: by 1870 the Middlesbrough furnaces could pour out 550 tons a day.

The capitalism of the times put a premium on production at all costs, and had little time to calculate social side effects—an attitude which made it many enemies. It was often prodigiously wasteful in its quest for maximum output: the coke ovens of County Durham poured 45,000 tons of sulphur into the sky every year during the 1880s, and the town of Coatbridge, Ayr, avoided the need for street lighting because of the nightly glow of the waste gases from its furnaces.

Refining iron into steel was an ancient and expensive craft which joined the ranks of factory production by a single technical breakthrough: the Bessemer converter (1856). The converter and its less dramatic rival, the open hearth furnace, were both expensive to build and operate, but the investment was usually justified because big markets awaited steel, a superior material to iron, for industrial use. It was used for rails (1860), ships (1863) and engineering in general, although its widespread adoption took some 20 years, mainly because of the unwillingness of ironfounders to scrap their expensive iron-founding machinery.

40

W. G. Armstrong (later Lord Armstrong) was one of the great mechanisers of the nineteenth century. He founded a heavy engineering complex on Tyneside. In 1859 he was Engineer of Rifle Ordnance at the Royal Arsenal, Woolwich (**34**). Here components are being made for his revolutionary breech-loading gun (1862).

This *managerial inertia* is another price paid for adopting a factory-based economy: capital 'sunk' in a factory and its plant represents sacrifice and risk, so entrepreneurs are often reluctant to 'junk' it before its useful life is over. This is understandable conservatism, but can prove very mischievous and bad business sense in a highly competitive and quickly changing world.

Much of the competition in steel came from abroad; by the end of the century

35 Armstrong's own works at Elswick (1887) was called 'an arsenal complete in itself' and contained 10 acres of steel works alone, plus private railways and warships on the stocks.

36 A National Projectile Factory in the First World War. The mass-production of munitions, often using female labour, was responsible for much social and industrial change, e.g. the widespread introduction of canteens and the final 'emancipation of women'. The ability of the State to erect and run such factories in a short time has become a vital factor in deciding the nature and outcome of modern war.

Great Britain had been overtaken by two rivals in the production of steel; Germany and the U.S.A.

	Output 1900, millions of tons
U.S.A.	13,500,000
German Empire	6,400,000
Great Britain	4,900,000

A growing market for steel was the armaments industry (**34**, **35**). The 'arms race' before the Great War, and the production of munitions in it (**36**) stimulated the steel industry as the Napoleonic war had provided markets for the iron-masters of Coalbrookdale and Merthyr Tydfil.

Clothing and Footwear

Production also changed from domestic to factory methods in the nineteenth century, mainly from 1850. In both trades the necessary invention was a sewing machine (invented by Howe 1844 and Singer 1851). A large market keenly awaited reasonably priced suits, blouses, shoes, etc., all of which were being machine made by 1914. Leeds was the first great centre of factory-produced clothing, Northampton of factory-made shoes. Towns like Wellingborough which relied on domestic methods declined, according to various Factory Reports at the turn of the century. One interesting by-product of these, the last, quickest and perhaps most obvious factory revolutions of that age, was the introduction of 'standard sizes' from the 1880s onwards, made necessary by mass-production and factory methods which do not cater for precise individual differences so easily as hand crafts.

Laundries

The cleaning of clothes and linen had traditionally been carried on by housewives or local washerwomen. The factory-laundry was developed in the late nineteenth century; from 1881 to 1911 the number of laundry workers rose from 3,600 to

37 A steam laundry, *c.* 1900: the wash house where clothes were washed *en masse* by factory methods.

Corner of Washhouse

13,000, while the traditional washerwomen fell in numbers from 189,000 to 180,000. A survey of London life before the First World War (*Living London*, ed. George Sims) described the mechanical equipment of laundries (**37**, **38**) thus: 'glorified washtubs, ingenious centrifugal driers, machines for "getting up" (i.e. finishing and ironing) ... weighing nearly 1,000 tons and worth about £50,000 ... a couple of decades back all the apparatus of a complete laundry could easily be put into a scullery; now many a metropolitan washing factory contains from £20,000 to £30,000 worth of machinery'.

38 The ironing room of a laundry resembled more a workshop than a factory because it contained a concentration of hand-ironing rather than mechanisation. The irons were heated by gas: note the connecting tubes and pipes.

39 A traditional paper mill at Wookey Hole, Somerset, *c.* 1890, dating from before 1610. Here paper was made by hand from raw materials which arrived by horse and cart.

Paper

The fate of textiles after their machine birth and machine washing described above might even be a machine death. One use for them devised in 1813 was being torn into *shoddy*, and thence woven into coarse cloth and cheap blankets. Another use was to employ rags in the manufacture of the finer grades of paper, another industry which grew from a domestic or workshop trade to a factory process in Victorian times.

Paper had been produced in workshops by hand-moulding pulp, ever since the Middle Ages. The innovation which introduced paper making into the factory age was the paper machine (in Britain after 1803). Its disarmingly prosaic name obscures its complexity and expense: by 1900 a single machine cost £10,000. These mass-producing machines were fed by the pulped wood of overseas forests, brought by steamships and fashioned in the mills into paper for the mass-markets of the industrial age: daily newspapers, office stationery etc. Overseas customers added to the demand which justified factory methods: in 1907 they bought 87,000 tons of paper out of the total output of 444,000 tons.

40 *(top right)* The paper machine revolutionised the industry. Here modern machines are housed in Bowater's Mill at Ellesmere Port, Cheshire.

41 *(bottom right)* Machines have called into existence the super-mill, which dwarfs earlier ones. This is the Kemsley Mill of Messrs Bowaters at Sittingbourne, Kent. Dating from 1924, it has its private dock and railway system, and operates six machines which convert pulp (from company-owned forests in Newfoundland) into paper for mass-produced newspapers. Thus from forest to morning paper, bulk transport and factory mass-production are the rule.

44

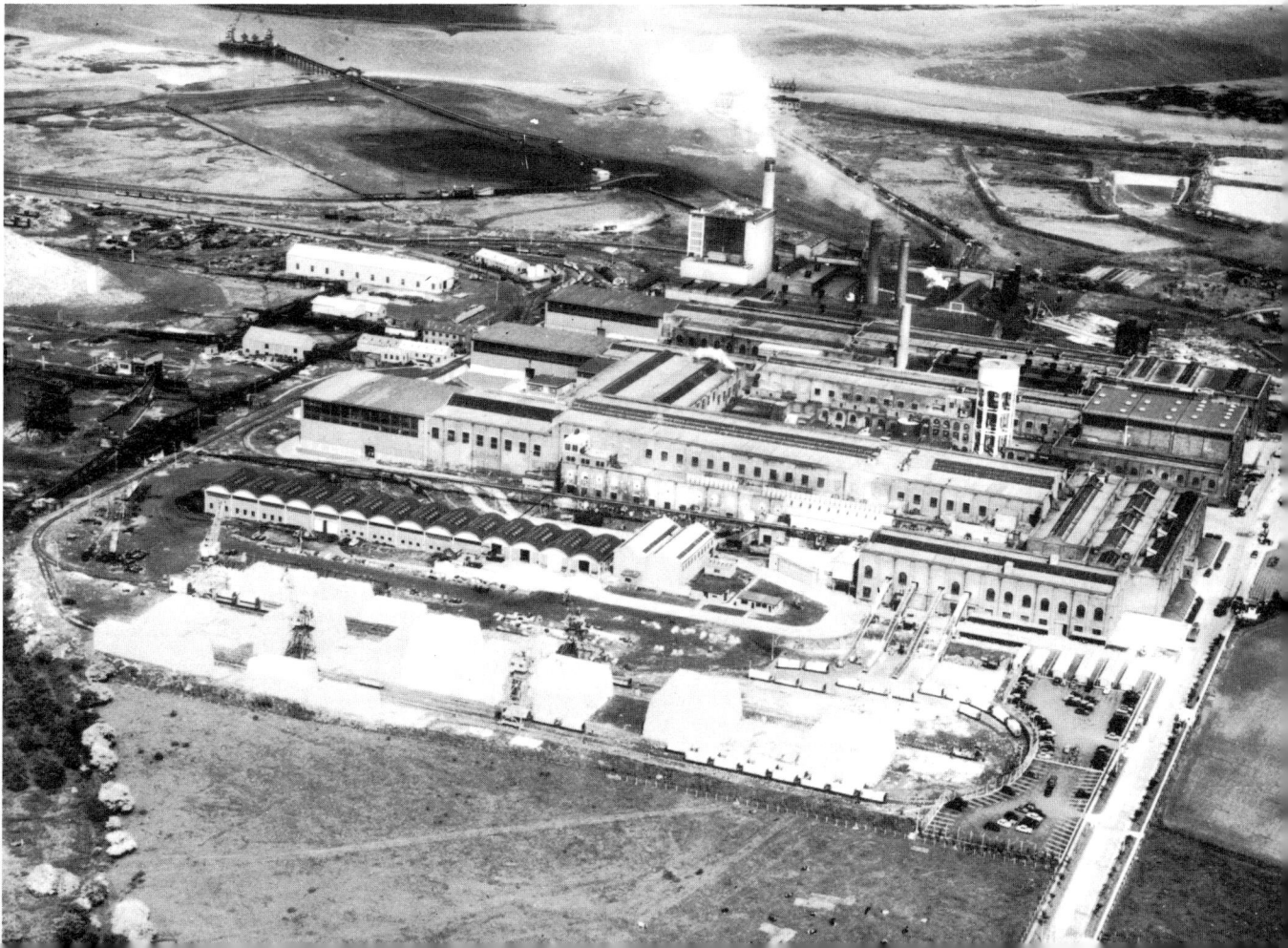

Factory production of biscuits (**42**) in 1926. Here they are being coated with sugar icing by a conveyor-belt process at the Liverpool works of Messrs W. & R. Jacobs.

These statistics show clearly (a) the decrease in the number of mills, (b) the vastly increased output per mill by (c) the employment of more machines: a classic case of the factory triumphant.

(a) *number of paper mills in Great Britain and Ireland*

1838	525
1907	207

(b) *amount of paper made (thousands of tons)*

	hand	machine	total
1800	11,300	—	11,300
1840	9,900	33,400	43,300
1800	3,500	286,000	289,500
1900	3,800	769,000	772,800

(c) *number of paper machines in Great Britain*

1810	17
1907	531

Factories and Food

The spread of the factory system created an army of critics who resented the loss of handicrafts and the personal touch. One of their favourite targets was the factory production of food. They feared the possibility of food adulteration and mass-poisoning from unclean factories. The self-interest of the manufacturers and (in later times) the most rigorously termed and carefully observed regulations have prevented these predictions from coming true. On the other hand, there were advantages to factory-processed food which appealed to the general public:

it was longer lasting than fresh food (especially attractive in the pre-refrigerator age), and was available throughout the year; there was also a richer variety of foods obtainable.

Mechanisation and factory production of some foods was established long before the Industrial Revolution: for instance windmills and watermills ground flour, breweries had fermented beer and ale centuries before the mills of Belper and Cromford were erected. The nineteenth century marked a sudden intensification and spread of this process to many foods and their component ingredients.

The factory production of *biscuits* is a good example (**42**). It resulted from growing markets and mechanical ingenuity, as with cotton textiles or paper manufacture. J. D. Carr, a baker of Carlisle, converted a printing machine into a primitive biscuit cutter, and found it to be more rapid and accurate in its work than hand cutters. He went on to develop his own flour mill at the nearby port of Silloth. By 1845 he was producing about 450 tons of biscuits a year, many carried to distant markets by rail. Methods of production have improved so much that a single machine can now make 6,000 tons of biscuits in a day. Nevertheless, the real change was in Carr's day, for then the principle of machine production was established: since then the process has merely been accelerated.

Flour milling changed in the nineteenth century. The picturesque windmills were unable to compete with the new steam roller-grinding mills which were set up in large ports to deal with overseas bulk supplies. By 1900 steam milling was dominant.

43 Factory production of sweets: like cigarettes, they were once hand-made, but in 1862 Henry I. Rowntree of York introduced a degree of mechanisation into the process. This encouraged standardisation, and Rowntree's 400 brands (1890) were reduced to a handful of highly popular ones by 1940. Here is hand-packing of chocolates (1936) giving an idea of the scale of the operation involved.

Tinned Food Factories

Like mechanical milling, preserving food is an ancient craft. In the Middle Ages meat was preserved by salting and spicing, although the consumption of such treated food was generally restricted to the upper strata of feudal society. Preserved food has proved invaluable for armies which have to be self-supporting, for expeditions cut off from supply bases, or for ordinary consumers who find packaged food convenient, purchasable throughout the year, and, unlike spiced meat, generally very palatable.

Factory-processed food, like baked beans and tinned jam, is now to be found in the majority of British households. Factory-baked bread, mass-produced biscuits and what is virtually factory-reared and treated farm produce—this encroachment of factory methods on to the people's diet is one of the most profound social changes arising from the factory system.

The first attempt to put food into portable preserving canisters was made by John Hall, an ironmaster of Dartford, and the versatile engineer, Bryan Donkin, f.r.s. (also the master-mind behind Foundrinier's paper mill, (p. 44)), who jointly erected a factory for containing food in canisters. It was built at Bermondsey, London, in 1802, and was stimulated by a single large market: the army then engaged in fighting France. Cooked food was placed in tinplate canisters. At the end of the French wars another customer was Ross's expedition to Baffin Bay (1814), and Parry's to the Arctic (1819); the surgeon of the latter found the tinned soups 'particularly excellent'.

The civilian market also grew after 1820, as more and various tinned canisters (usually corrupted to 'tin cans' or simply 'tins' of food) appeared on the market, where they were sometimes sold under the bizarre euphemism of 'embalmed provisions'. Further technical developments encouraging this trend were the automatic tin can punching machine (1847) and safer and quicker cooking by pressure-cooker (1874). Tins were widely employed to carry biscuits, sweets, chocolates and tobacco as well as the many standard canned foods

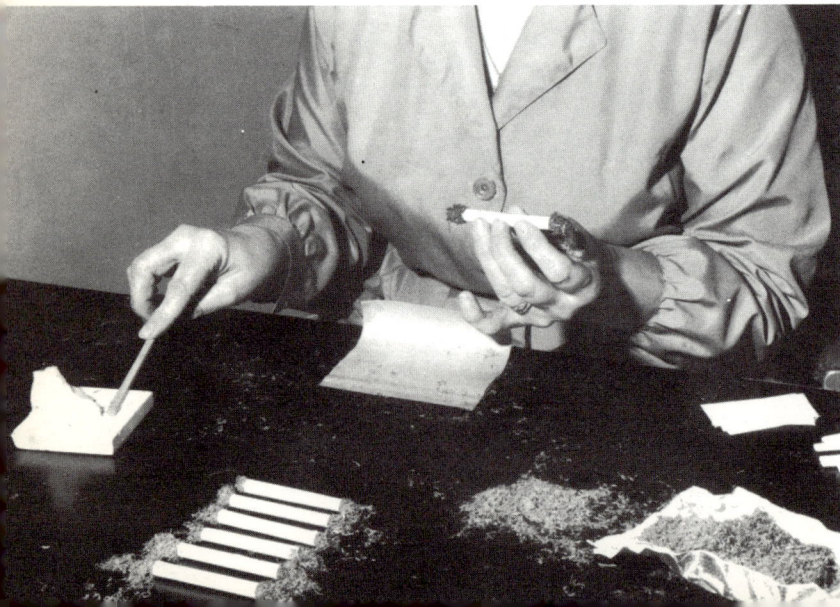

44 Hand production of cigarettes: here pasting is taking place prior to trimming.

45 Cigarette machines meant a less personal touch but higher productivity. This 1914 photograph was taken at the Bristol works of Messrs W. D. & H. O. Wills.

The inter-relationship of the tinplate industry and food preserving is obvious, and it is important to note again the part played by war in accelerating economic development. In the present century the process of employing factory methods in food processing has gone even further. Milk is bottled in giant dairies: cows are even milked mechanically. Butter and cheese are processed and wrapped by factory methods. A factory-based frozen-food industry has grown since 1945.

Agriculture is itself referred to as an 'industry', because elements of factory production have appeared in farming, in for instance the erection of 'broiler farms' for the concentrated rearing of poultry in special buildings. Writing in *The Channel Islands*, Wilfred Hooke says of the intensive vegetable farming there: '. . . there is no real waste land on the farms. They are in fact "factories" with a high production schedule to be maintained. . . .' This development is quite common in much of British agriculture, and its early origins were noted by Cobbett (pp. 11–12). In this way one of civilisation's oldest occupations has been transformed by factory methods.

Cigarettes

Ever since its adoption by Europeans in the sixteenth century, tobacco had been smoked in pipes. In the nineteenth century the more convenient cigarette (a native of continental Europe) became popular in Britain (*c.* 1850 onwards) but was hand made (**44**) in shops or workshops. Factory production started in 1883 when the Bristol tobacco merchants, Messrs W. D. & H. O. Wills, bought two American-made cigarette machines. The industry had relied on handworkers (technically it was labour-intensive), now machines did most of the work (i.e. capital-intensive). Each machine produced 100,000 cigarettes a day. The old cry of alarm at the death of hand-production was heard as in so many other industries which converted to factory production. A trade magazine (1885) reported a visit to Messrs Gallaher of Belfast, then still employing hand-rollers; these girls produced 'cigarettes all made by hand, as it is considered that being thus made, they are superior to those made mechanically'.

This skill (not so ancient as most supplanted by factories) could not compete with the mass-production of popular brands which Wills offered the public, e.g. 'Woodbines' (1888). Not all sections of the public approved of the habit, for instance a slightly shocked correspondent of the *Birmingham Gazette* (1887): 'three young ladies entered a railway carriage and proceeded to light cigarettes in public . . . the calm audacity of the proceeding showed that the girls, though young, were practised smokers . . .'. Once more, the factories had accelerated a social revolution.

Brewing

The brewing of beer is a far older industry than the making of cigarettes, but it, too, had fallen into the hands of factory producers by 1900. Until the eighteenth century it was the rule to brew beer at home. One hears of ale and beer brewed by Scottish farmers 'so new that it was scarce cold when it was brought to the table'. Elsewhere, beer was brewed by publicans in their own taverns ('brewing victuallers'); the general brewer willing to sell beer in bulk to any buyer (called a 'common brewer') was rare. Yet economic facts were on the side of the common brewer: he could take advantage of large-scale technical developments, such as steam pumps, which his smaller rivals could not. One such brewer was John Rigg of Aberdeen; the first common brewer of the city who gave it ale 'at a cheaper and better quality than they can possibly manufacture it themselves'. The 'they' referred to the domestic brewers, who had almost vanished 14 years after Rigg started (1765).

In 1700 there were 750 common brewers; 100 years later there were 1,400. By 1750 the 12 largest common brewers of London produced half of all common brewers' output; a remarkably early example of concentration. Brewing victuallers could not compete with this and steadily declined: in 1700 there were 40,000 of them; in 1800 there were 24,000 and in 1886, 12,000.

46 The first modern dye-works; Perkin's colour factory, as it was called, at Greenford Green, Middlesex (1873). It was started in 1856 by the first man to fix such colours as mauve (1856); magenta (so named by him, 1859) and turkey red (1869)—all derivatives of coal tar, and all used by the textile industry.

In all these ways the factory system has come to dominate the production, processing and packaging of food and drink. The future holds possibilities of carrying this further; society is promised dehydrated foods, and even artificial foods produced from petrochemicals. The spread of the factory system in the food industries is not yet complete from a world point of view, although dominant in certain economically advanced states. It will one day probably be the universal rule if the pressure of population on the world's limited resources continues.

Chemicals

One of the fastest growing activities in the industrial era has been the production of chemicals. It was encouraged by the growth of the cotton textile industry in the late eighteenth century. Two processes in particular benefited from this: bleaching (whitening finished cloth) and dyeing (colouring it). Traditional bleaching was a non-factory industry, for the most part carried out in Holland, near Haarlem, where the cloth was treated in potash and buttermilk and left exposed throughout the summer. It was returned, whitened by this method, every autumn.

Such a roundabout and expensive process was another bottleneck preventing the fullest possible use of the factory system. A few bleach fields were laid out in the British Isles, notably in Galloway (1728), and the application of sulphuric acid in place of milk (1746) speeded the matter. The true breakthrough was the employment of chlorine gas from the mid-1780s. By this new method the cloth was exposed in large chlorine chambers; but the pungent, even fatal, chlorine gas rendered the innovation unpopular. A safer way was to use bleaching powder, discovered by Charles Tennant of Glasgow (1799). This was the real birth of the 'heavy' chemical industry: the production on a large scale of acids and alkalis for industrial use.

From its birth the heavy chemical industry required expensive plant. Chemical works are a type of factory, especially designed around the processes that take place within. Tennant's works at St Rollox, Glasgow, were the largest chemical establishment in the world by 1830. The production of some chemicals created various by-products. Occasionally these were exploited commercially, but too many, in those early days, were allowed to run away as 'effluent', poisoning rivers, or blighting the countryside. The adoption of the Leblanc process for obtaining

51

Heavy chemicals: **47** *(left)* the Winnington works of Brunner, Mond & Co. (now part of I.C.I.) about 1884. Here caustic soda and its by-products have been made for over eighty years. **48** *(right)*

alkali (sodas) from 1823 onwards led to many useful by-products being created in quantity, including sodium carbonate (washing soda), hydrochloric acid and the all-important bleaching powder. Broadly speaking, the basis of this manufacture was the roasting of common salt, vast quantities of which lay under the ground in Cheshire, where the industry was centred (**47**).

By 1864, 38 out of Britain's 84 soda works were in South Lancashire or North Cheshire—extremely convenient to the cotton textile industry. The £3 million of capital invested in the Leblanc process (1883) was the main reason why its superior successor, the Solvay process, was slow in introduction: another example of inertia in the factory system, and of the penalties attendant on Britain being the first state to industrialise, and therefore the one most likely to be weighed down with out-dated equipment.

The chemical industry found it hard to obtain capital, which was being sunk instead in cotton, coal and overseas speculation. All these recipients were to prove disastrous risks in the future.

Other heavy chemical production associated with the Industrial Revolution were sulphuric acid (then called 'oil of vitriol') and alum. Before industrial times,

52

encrusted machinery with attendant pipes and container casks in the 'ash shed' (i.e. soda ash) at Winnington, c. 1890.

sulphuric acid had been used by tanners, paper makers, metal workers and others. It was made in a few small works such as those of Joshua Ward, where his partner, Mr White, described as an 'ingenious chymist' who 'carries on the Great Vitriol Works at Twickenham', so offended the local inhabitants by the strong smells issuing from the works that he had to shut down. More important was the works of Roebuck and Garbett (1746) in the metal-working district of Birmingham. The use of sulphuric acid in bleaching created the demand necessary to justify large-scale acid factories: by 1797 Glasgow had eight to serve the Lanarkshire cotton industry, and in 1820 England had 24 such works.

Alum was important in the textile finishing trade as a 'mordant' in vegetable dyestuffs. In connexion with woollen textiles in the pre-industrial age, it is known that an alum works was set up at Whitby, Yorkshire, in the reign of Elizabeth I. The Industrial Revolution needed alum on a generous scale, and true factory production was started by Charles Macintosh at Hurlet near Paisley (1797) and at Campsie, Stirlingshire (1808). A contemporary seeing the latter wrote of considerable chemical works where alum . . . Prussian blue (a dye) &c are manu-factured on an extensive scale; and in which a very large capital appears to be

53

embarked'. In 1812 this works turned out 1,000 tons of alum a year, and in 1835, 2,000 tons. By the standards of the time this was production on a grand scale, and further evidence of the power and efficacy of the factory system.

Soap

Nineteenth-century Britain needed large amounts of soap for the most obvious reasons: more people; more dirt to wash off because of the industrial filth of the atmosphere; better standards of personal hygiene and more money available to buy soap as the century wore on, turning it from a luxury into an everyday necessity.

The manufacture of soap had always been domestic, although some cities were large enough to justify a local soapworks. Soap was made by boiling together olive oil, tallow, ashes and lime, and allowing the resulting mixture to cool. Such a process lends itself well to factory methods, but it was not worth investing in these until demand grew sufficiently. The repeal of the old soap duty (1853)—

49 A soap factory: the pan room at the Lever Bros. works at Port Sunlight (1900) where fat and alkali were combined to make some of Levers' famous products—Sunlight Soap, Lifebuoy (1894) and Lux Soapflakes (1899).

Brick production came into the factory system in the nineteenth century. **50** shows the hand production of bricks common in 1800, but quite inadequate for the scale of supply required in modern society.

castigated as a 'tax on cleanliness'—and the arrival of piped water in many urban areas spurred on the demand which was based, originally, on the factors listed above. Consumption rose markedly:

1801 : 24,000 tons   1841 : 75,000 tons   1891 : 260,000 tons

and, whereas in 1801 the average person used 3·6 lb. of soap a year, he or she used 15·4 lb. in 1891: an interesting index of civilisation.

Such conditions are ideal for factory production, providing raw materials are available in sufficient quantities. The exploitation of new sources of oil (West Africa) and tallow (Australia), and their carriage in steamships completed the

51 shows a part of the mechanised brick works of A. Boulton & Co. at Wellington in Shropshire, dating from the 1850s. Such works and slate quarries helped house the people and industries of the Victorian age.

pattern of necessary conditions. At first manufacturers (many of them concentrated in the Cheshire–Lancashire chemical belt) merely met the new demand as it arose.

The peculiar element of the successful soap entrepreneurs was their massive use of 'marketing' (like Josiah Wedgwood) to create new demand, rather than simply responding to casual growth.

Most famous of the publicisers of the virtues of soap was the firm of Lever Bros. Lever appreciated the necessity of a vast 'market of the people' and set out to cultivate and educate it. The factory and adjacent factory-owned town which benefited from this marketing was Port Sunlight (1889). Lever told the public that soap was a necessity of life, and kept the names of his standard mass-produced brands (**49**) before them by means of advertisements in newspapers, on railway stations and in shops. He offered prizes for collected packet tops (wrongly believed to be a trick of modern marketing) and so increased business that Port Sunlight employed 6,000 by 1911 and justified the sanguine faith of its founder.

There is, in Lever's story, as in Arkwright's or Armstrong's, an heroic quality, manifest in their great mills and works: hives of activity which enriched civilisation in many ways. Yet many contemporaries of Lever (e.g. Ruskin and William Morris) were depressed by the squalor which accompanied the factory system, which seemed to degrade humanity. Their evidence was vague and selective, but it contained much truth. Not all factory owners were so benevolent as Lever or Salt (**11**) who built company towns and treated their employees as a family. Few employees wept over the death of their employer as did those of John Bright, a factory-owner and statesman of Rochdale.

However, for all the horror of the system there was *hope*. Men like Lever showed that factories and a factory-based civilisation did not have to mean eternal poverty and grime. On the contrary, factories provided the key of escape; for the first time in 7,000 or more years there was a good chance that the masses of ordinary people might have leisure and holidays, and purchase luxuries—no small miracle, especially in view of the great size and rapid growth of the population.

Reading List

Sir John Clapham: *Economic History of Modern Britain (Vol. I–III)*
J. D. Chambers: *The Workshop of the World*
J. D. Scott: *Vickers, a History*
S. G. Checkland: *The Rise of Industrial Society in Britain*
A. Dykes Spicer: *The Paper Trade*
Samuel Smiles: *Industrial Biography*
Dictionary of National Biography: especially sections on Lord Armstrong, Lord Leverhulme and Sir Titus Salt

4 Factories and Society

Although individual factories had been known before the Industrial Revolution, they had been rare and isolated: objects of curiosity. Now they came in legions: nothing like this had been seen in recorded history—a civilisation living by manufacture with ever smaller proportions of the population engaged in agriculture. The nature and pace of the change baffled contemporaries: the ruling élite of landowning nobility and gentry were peculiarly unprepared; the growing urban middle class clamoured for political power to match its new economic status. The greatest problem lay in the largest class of the industrial age: the working class, at once enigmatic and threatening.

In two centuries Great Britain has learnt to accept factories and industrialism, and perhaps understand something of them. Only an optimist could claim that in the years between Richard Arkwright and the present day society has mastered the industrial system and its side effects.

The Factories and Labour

Traditionally, the most notorious aspect of the early factories was their employment of children. But this was by no means new: children had been widely employed under the domestic system. The factories concentrated this fact for all to see, and added refinements of brutality (in some cases) which came readily to the public notice.

A legend attributed to the French historian, Jules Michelet, has it that William Pitt (Prime Minister at the time of the Industrial Revolution) replied to some factory owners who complained to him about the high wages they had to pay: 'take the children'. In fact, he said in a House of Commons speech (1796): 'Experience has already shown how much could be done by the industry of children, and the advantages of early employing them in such branches of manufactures as they are able to execute.' The 'experience' to which Pitt referred was the centuries-old tradition of employing children, such as the traveller Defoe noted in early eighteenth-century Yorkshire: 'We saw the Houses (domestic wool industry) full of lusty fellows, some at the Dye-vat, some at the loom . . .; the women and children carding and spinning . . . scarce any thing above four years old but its hands were sufficient for its own support.'

What Pitt and his contemporaries were not aware of was the big difference between working in the atmosphere of one's own family and, on the other hand, in a mill owned by an unknown employer, particularly if the millowner in question was a profiteer who drove labour hard. Another matter hidden from Pitt was the grinding monotony of some factory labour, the overheated and fluffy air of the textile mills, the poor light and seemingly endless hours of work to which the unfortunate children were subjected.

Child labour came from two sources: poor families who 'farmed' out their children and were glad to add another wage-earner to their number; and apprentices. The 'apprentices' were really children of poor parents who were either unemployed or dead. Under the laws of the time these children were fed and kept by local parish authorities. Densely populated London had thousands of these pauper children 'on the rates'. The new cotton mills of the North were able to use children to work the fairly unsophisticated machinery: water frames, mules, etc. A bargain was struck between the parishes and the millowners: the latter would relieve the former of the children, and give them employment between the ages of 7 and 21 as 'apprentices' or trainees. The millowners did not have to pay them; merely house, train and feed them. For up to 14 years they would toil for 15 hours every day, sleep in shifts in a mill dormitory and on Sunday, the 'day of rest', they cleaned and oiled the factory machinery—the only part of the system which did relax.

John Fielden wrote in his book *The Curse of the Factory System* (1836) that these children were 'harassed to the brink of death by excessive labour . . . starved to the bone while flogged to work. . . . The beautiful and romantic valleys of Derbyshire, Nottinghamshire and Lancashire, secluded from the public eye, became the dismal solitudes of torture.' He attacked the greedy millowners who 'began the practice of "night working" . . . having tired out one set of hands by working them throughout the day, they had another set ready to go on working through the night; the day set getting into the beds the night set had just quitted. . . . It is a common tradition in Lancashire that the beds *never got cold*.'

A man giving official evidence in 1833, recollected seeing children 'tumble down asleep among . . . the machinery, and so get cruelly hurt.' The same man had been carted up from London as a pauper boy from the parish of St Pancras, crowded with others in two large waggons, like cattle, and given: 'milk porridge of a very blue complexion' and 'bread partly made of rye—very black and so soft that they could scarcely swallow it, as it stuck like bird lime to the teeth'. (*A memoir of Robert Blincoe, an Orphan boy; . . . sent to endure the horrors of a Cotton Mill,* 1832.) A parliamentary enquiry (1816) contained this exchange:

Question: Were any children injured by the machinery?

Answer: Very frequently. Very often their fingers were crushed. . . .

Q: Were any of the children deformed?

A: Yes, several; there were two or three that were very crooked.

On the other hand, some children clearly received humane treatment, a fact which suggests that the brutality referred to above cannot be called 'normal', although one mill operated on such lines would constitute a moral wrong, then

52 'In the East of Scotland many . . . girls . . . carrying coals on their backs up steep ladders': so said the *Children's Employment Commission* (1842). An unpleasant accident seems imminent in this picture from the official report.

and now. At a mill in New Lanark, Scotland, the children were dressed in woollens, the girls had best dresses for Sunday, and all had nearly $1\frac{1}{2}$ lb. of fresh beef and 5 oz. of cheese for supper with plenty of potatoes and bread.

Public discovery of the scandalous conditions in some mills led to one of the first attempts by the state, in modern times, to curb the extreme exploitation of poor children by factory owners: the *Health and Morals of Apprentices Act* (1802), described in the section **The Factory Acts** (p. 71). It is believed that 20,000 apprentices had been employed under this iniquitous system at its peak, *c.* 1800.

The 1802 Act came as the apprentice system was decaying in any case. New forms of child exploitation were growing in the cotton towns. Here the hand-loom weavers, suffering acute poverty in competition with the steam-driven factories, sent their children into those very factories to earn extra money for the family. The factory owner did not even have the trouble of feeding and clothing this new army, he merely drove them the same 5.00 a.m. to 8.00 p.m. day, six days a week. Meal time, so termed, consisted of snatching a sandwich while oiling machinery.

The conditions of these 'wage-slaves' were as odious as those of the apprentices. When 'rush orders' were on, the mill might start at 3.00 a.m.; punishments were liberally awarded for lateness or slackness. The oppressive monotony of tending a spinning mule for fifteen hours per day was punishment enough; another official witness (1832) recollected this pathetic conversation between a six-year-old boy and his father when both were working in a cotton mill: 'Father, what o'clock is it?' 'Seven o'clock.' 'Oh, is it two hours to nine o'clock? I cannot bear it.' His attitude is hardly surprising when it is remembered that tending a textile machine might involve twenty miles of to-and-fro pacing every day. Another law, the *Factory Act (1819)*, attempted to deal with the plight of wage-earning children, but it was a failure.

The children forced to work in cotton mills were given some protection by the *Factory Act (1833)*; other children, working in coal mines and various other industries were not afforded equal protection for some years. An official report on children working in coal mines (1842) exposed more horrors: four-year-olds working underground, children up to thirteen working ventilation traps in total darkness for twelve hours per day (**52**). The report drew attention to the frequency of underground accidents, not a few caused by entrusting steam winding-gear to inexperienced boys.

On the other hand, there seemed little brutality or deliberate exploitation such as was found in the cotton mills; much employment in coal mines was on a family basis. However, the report condemned the system thoroughly, and since its terms of reference covered tin, lead, copper and zinc mining, all these joined coal mining in the *Mines Act (1842)* which forbade the employment of children underground. No more would children suffer like Mary Davis a 'very pretty little girl' from South Wales: 'her lamp had gone out for want of oil, she said rats or some one had run away with her bread and cheese . . .' or Sarah Gooder (8) 'I have to trap without a light, and I'm scared. Sometimes I sing when I have a light, but not in the dark, I dare not sing then.'

Children in general manufacture had to wait until the *Factory Act (1847)* for protection, when legal limits were prescribed for their hours of work. A report of the Children's Employment Commission (1843) told the same story again, of young children (as young as three) working sometimes eighteen hours per day, of exploited 'apprentices'; of 'deformity of the limbs and diseases of the lungs', of hands and fingers jammed in unguarded gear-wheels or 'drawn in between rollers'. One commissioner saw a workshop where pins were made in Broad Street, Birmingham, where an overseer strode about with a cane smacking children who relaxed, and where there was one foul lavatory for 100 children. Another report noted small boys hammering heated iron into nails, no terrible task in itself, save that the hours of work were 5.00 a.m. to 11.00 p.m.! At another nail-works a boy making bad nails was liable to be hung upside down from the ceiling. Although many of these incidents of sadism occurred in workshops, it is clear that the absence of proper factory law and inspection led to a situation whereby any place of work, domestic or mechanised, could be a chamber of horrors.

The commissioners also found decent workshops and factories, but, although pleasing, it did not excuse maltreatment elsewhere. Even an increasingly enlightened public saw nothing intrinsically evil in child labour as such. W. Cooke Taylor, in *Factories and the Factory System* (1844) thought: 'we would rather see boys and girls earning their means of support in the mill than starving by the road side, shivering on pavements, or conveyed to Bridewell . . .' (a prison). Sir Edward Baines, writing of the textile industry (1837), while he admitted that the work might be dull and unhealthy, still found the children 'more sportive than gloomy' and used to the din which overwhelmed the casual visitor. Dr Ure, always very biassed towards the employers, wrote (1835) that he never saw 'children in ill humour' in the factories of Manchester, rather 'the work of these lively elves seemed to resemble a sport, in which habit gave them a pleasing dexterity'. He claimed that the children ran out of the mill at the end of the day 'with the same alacrity as boys issuing from a school'—which might mean they were glad to get away, or that they were full of *joie de vivre*.

Despite the claims of such men as Baines and Ure, many factories of the time were houses of cruelty and misery. Even the more brutal world of the 1830s knew and felt this. The fact that some employers were kind was gratifying, but irrelevant. In spite of specious arguments produced to justify the system, Parliament determined to stop it, and by degrees it was destroyed. The sacrifice of children was the first, and perhaps the greatest, evil of the factory system.

Female Labour and the Factories

The employment of small children has long been illegal in Great Britain. On the other hand, the employment of women is not; in fact, they supply a large and valuable part of the national work force. As in the case of children, they had worked from time immemorial at many tasks. The arrival of the factory system, however, changed the aspect of female labour. Women now worked away from the family circle, becoming employees rather than partners. Like children they were driven hard in a way that struck many people as brutal and degrading. On the other hand, becoming wage earners was the first stage in making women genuinely independent. This 'emancipation of women' has been a long process and is still unfinished. It has had profound social effects, for instance, the 'working mother' whose work takes her away from the home: a phenomenon that appeared first in Lancashire in the textile mills areas.

As in the case of the children, there were diverse views on the question of female labour. There was a clear necessity for legislation when the evidence was weighed, and female labour was duly protected, e.g. the *Factory Act (1847)*. One writer, P. Gaskell in his *Manufacturing Population of England* (1833) made some uncharitable observations about factory girls: 'Here . . . will be found an utter absence of grace and feminine manners—a peculiar raucous or rough timbre of voice . . . no delicacy of figure . . . no "heaven within her eye" . . . but in their place an awkward and ungainly figure, limbs badly moulded from imperfect nutrition'. Their work; he felt made them walk with 'a sort of waddle . . . this gait may be detected in great numbers of factory girls and women'. Even if these sour remarks had any basis in fact, it is pleasing to learn from other more chivalrous writers, that while 'Factory labour does not indeed improve the form or complexion . . . it is less injurious to either than many of the ordinary employments of females . . . Lancashire has its fair proportion of beautiful women, and the factories have not yet abated its ancient fame for the witchery of female charms' (W. Cooke Taylor). Dr Ure, mentioned above, in his *The Philosophy of Manufactures* (1835) remarked on the graceful posture, Grecian good looks and 'tasteful modes of wearing neat handkerchiefs on their heads' of many of the mill girls. The 1833 government investigation alluded to the neat attire of factory girls of independent means (i.e. earning wages): such as 18-year-old 'Jane L' who earned 16s. per week, gave her mother 7s., owned and made a number of 'becoming garments'. (**53**)

For those who pined for the old days of handicrafts which had been displaced by the 'Satanic Mills', the official report on the hand-loom weavers (1840) reminded everyone that 'one of the greatest advantages resulting from the progress of manufacturing industry, and from severe manual labour being superseded by machinery, is its tendency to raise the condition of women'. A factory girl, the report stated, might save £100 between the ages of 16 and 25 towards her marriage, and she need not be 'driven into early marriage by the necessity of seeking a home'.

Female labour was found mainly in the textile mills; other factory industries (until the advent of modern light industry) generally required work which was too heavy for women, although coal mines certainly employed them at one time (see below). Factory wives were a large proportion of the female labour force in the mills (1834):

60,000 adult males	43,000 boys below 18
65,000 adult females	41,000 girls below 18

Frederick Engels, an employer and social theorist (also close friend of Karl Marx, the founder of Communism), made the interesting estimate that (in the mid-1830s) nearly 11,000 married women worked in the cotton mills, and that half of their husbands were so employed. These women were away from home at least twelve hours a day, which was a corrosive influence on family life. Many appeared not to know the rudiments of cooking, sewing, etc. Evidence to the Factory Commission (1833) claimed that they were 'brought up in the factory

53 *Dinner Hour at Wigan*, by Eyre Crowe: some of Lancashire's famous mill girls, whose shawls and clogs were symbols of the factory age. In the pre-canteen era workpeople like these girls left the mill for a midday meal, enjoying their legal right to do so under the Factory Act, 1847.

until they are married, and sometimes working long after that event has taken place, even when they have become mothers, they are almost entirely ignorant of household duties'. Evidence at a later date (1842) talked of a Birmingham mother of eleven children who 'worked in a manufactory from an early age' and who 'made many efforts to abstain from shop (i.e. factory) work; but her pecuniary necessities forced her back . . .'. She was known 'after the close of a hard day's work (to) sit up nearly all night for several nights together washing and mending clothes'. Like many wives of the Industrial Revolution she had to bear with a husband who drank heavily: the connexion between this vice ('intemperance' as it was termed) and the factory system is dealt with later (p. 81).

The real scandal of female labour was the employment of women in coal mines. The North-East coal field had stopped this practice in the 1780s, but it was common in Scotland and could be found in Cumberland, Lancashire and South Wales. As in the case of child labour, all kinds of casuistry were produced to justify the system. The coal owners were adept at producing evidence to counter the humanitarians who supported the 1842 Mines Bill. Their point of view failed to stop the bill, and it became an Act. Among the interests supporting female labour were some of the male pitmen who told a Parliamentary enquiry (1842) that women were 'better to manage' and kept time better. From the employer's point of view a 20-year-old girl 'will work for 2s. a day or less, and a man of that age will want 3s. 6d.' Women who could carry heavy coal baskets were, incidentally, eyed as potentially hardy wives.

These attitudes failed to alter the general impression of horrid and un-feminine toil. The engineer Robert Bald (1812) wrote of women climbing down one of the coal mines of Scotland, a lit candle in their teeth, twenty-four times per day, bearing 170 lb. of coal in a basket up a 117-foot wooden ladder on the upward journey. Some women carried over two tons of coal each day! Such might be their life until they were fifty or sixty years old—every day to 'return home where no comfort awaits them; their clothes are frequently soaked with water and covered with mud . . . the cold . . . freezing their clothes . . . on getting home the fire is generally out, the culinary utensils dirty and unprepared'. Little wonder that one such woman sighed in despair to the engineer, 'O Sir, this is sore, sore work. I wish to God the first woman who tried to bear coal had broken her back and none would have tried it again.' Richard Ayton (1813) descended the William Pitt mine near Whitehaven, Cumberland, and was shocked by women 'of extraordinary wretchedness . . . blackened all over with dirt, and altogether so miserably disfigured . . . that they looked like a race fallen from the common rank of men, and doomed, in a kind of purgatory, to wear away their lives in these dismal shades.'

This tragic race of women was spirited away from 'these dismal shades' by the *Mines Act (1842)*. There is evidence that some women disobeyed this Act—not their employers—and secretly worked underground to raise the apparent output of their husbands (who were paid *piece-rates*, i.e. by results). Mr Robert Smith, mineral agent of Blaenavon Colliery (Monmouthshire), had a work force of 900; even after the 1842 Act he discovered 70 females illegally at work, a score of them were below eleven years old. Like many other collieries, Blaenavon tried to find pithead work for the ex-pitwomen, e.g. sorting and loading coal. The fact that some women returned voluntarily to 'the shades' shows that the practice of employing females underground had some natural basis in an age of very low wages. The introduction of machinery in coal mines for winding coals to the surface was already replacing female labour. The law merely accelerated this desirable economic process.

The Working Class

The workers who operated the factories, mills and railways of industrial Britain were a new social group: the working class. They must be distinguished from the varieties of rural 'plain men' of old: yeomen, copyholders, squatters, etc., who had lived close to nature, leased or owned land, and led lives rich in tradition and custom. The factory worker owned no land, very probably lived in an urban slum and depended on mysterious economic forces for his livelihood. If the trading cycle (succession of good times and bad) was against him he might starve, for he owned not even a cabbage patch to sustain his family and himself. His relationship with his employer was a purely monetary one—a 'cash nexus' as Thomas Carlyle put it. The factory owner was no local patron like the traditional squire or laird; his responsibility was to pay for work done, no more. If business was bad, employees were sacked.

As noted before, there were many excellent and benevolent employers: Oastler, Fielden, Salt, etc.; even Arkwright had built his workers plain but substantial dwellings. Nor were the squires of Old England always so solicitous concerning the local poor as later anti-industrial propaganda implied. Enclosing land, like factories, brought efficiency and raised the standard of living of all— in the long run. Both processes generated much social unrest; very few societies, if any, have discovered the secret of painless modernisation. Britain was the first to feel the ill-effects of material progress.

There had once been a state and social code for industry. One of its pillars was the guild system. A guild was a voluntary association of employers and employees which flourished in the Middle Ages. It attempted to regulate standards of quality, profits, wages, etc. The masters of Tudor and Stuart times found ways of avoiding this already decaying system, for instance, by carrying on their work outside the borough boundaries where the guild had no influence. By the time the factory system came the guilds were dead, and afforded no protection to the workers.

The state had attempted to take up the work of the guilds in their latter and failing days. This spirit of 'state paternalism' was enshrined in the *Statute of Artificers* (1563) which was a comprehensive series of regulations relating to wages, conditions of apprenticeship and so on. This and other statutes remained the law of the land for centuries, and although obsolescent and frequently ignored, they were a possible check on factory owners in the new age.

The employers, on the other hand, insisted that any interference in the running of their mills and works was wrong; it would destroy the 'sanctity of free contract' between 'free' men. It might have been possible to counter such bogus arguments (e.g. how was a starving apprentice a 'free man'?) but for the extraordinary power of economic philosophy over men's minds. One of the most masterful economists of all time, Lord Keynes, said: 'Practical men, who believe themselves to be quite exempt from any intellectual influences, are usually the slaves of some defunct economist.'

The dominant economist at the time of the Industrial Revolution (and by no means 'defunct') was Adam Smith, whose work *An Inquiry into the Nature and Causes of the Wealth of Nations*, 1776 (usually referred to by the last three words of the title), was to govern economic thought for many years. Smith argued that economies took care of themselves, as if what he called a 'hidden hand' kept all activity in a magic balance. State meddling upset natural tendencies and did mischief. His attitude (usually called *laissez-faire*: French for 'let alone') was strongly held by many important men of affairs in the age when Britain was the workshop of the world.

Armed with this philosophy, which they held with dogmatic obstinacy, the factory owners lobbied the government to scrap the old Elizabethan protective codes. The government obliged, and most of the laws were repealed 1809–15. At the same time, Parliament was persuaded to pass new laws which were influenced by Smith's doctrines. For instance the *Combination Laws* (1799 and 1800) which made any combination likely to 'restrain trade' henceforth illegal. It was meant to apply to bands of both employers and workers, but in practice it referred to the latter only and so stifled early trade unions. Thus the workers had no protection: guilds were dead, old statutes were defunct or repealed, and new laws militated against them.

Sections of the working class struck back. Between 1811 and 1817 times were especially hard for the working class: prices were high, but wages lagged behind. A series of violent industrial outbreaks (called *Luddism*) occurred. Luddism usually manifested itself in machine-breaking, although it was more than a purely anti-factory movement. There were three outbreaks: in the West Riding, Nottinghamshire and Lancashire. In Yorkshire, Luddism was an attempt of 'croppers' (finishers of woollen cloth) to stop machines, such as gig mills and shearing frames, replacing them. Similar trouble had already occurred in the West Country's declining wool industry. It had long been suspected that Yorkshire would suffer such trouble, for instance a Wiltshire soldier wrote to his M.P. (1802): 'We know that it has been mentioned to our great men . . . in Parliament by them that have factories how many poor they employ, forgetting . . . how many more they would employ were they to have it done by hand as they used to . . . I am informed by many that there will be a Revolution. . . . The burning of Factorys . . . we know is not right, but starvation forces Nature to do that which he would not.'

Yorkshire's first steam mill in the woollen industry was greeted by the jeers of hostile crowds. Among the enemies of large-scale mechanisation were the smaller masters, i.e. owners of modest workshops, or clothiers who relied upon the domestic system and observed (1795): 'of late several merchants . . . have erected very large buildings which are called Factories, wherein they intend to employ clothiers as their servants, so that persons (formerly employed in the domestic system) will be . . . in a dependent state'.

In the spirit of *laissez-faire*, Parliament swept away a mass of old laws protecting woollen hand-crafts (1809). 'The way was now open for the factory, the gigmill . . . the employment of unskilled and juvenile labour. The road to *any* constitutional redress was finally blocked. The croppers replied to the factories and machines

54 The Black Country: an early industrial view, showing the forges and smelters of the 'Workshop of the World', such as impressed Dickens and John Martin (p. 84). This landscape seemed the absolute opposite of traditional rural England, hence its disquieting effect on some observers.

by attacks on those hated aspects of the new world, claiming leadership emanated from a mythical "Ned Ludd" as they termed him "General of the Army of Redressers".' (E. P. Thompson.)

In Nottinghamshire Luddism arose from the resentment of framework knitters and small masters of workshops against those masters who had introduced the wide-frame to mass-produce inferior gloves, stockings, etc. The Luddite outbursts of 1811–12 broke up £10,000 worth of these frames. Parliament evidently did not see this as the 'hidden hand' and passed a bill (1812) making machine-breaking a capital offence. Later in the year it refused to protect the traditional knitters when they presented a petition.

In Lancashire Luddism was the response of hand-loom weavers to powered factories and mass-produced textiles which were ruining old handicrafts. They asked Parliament for a fixed legal minimum wage: 40,000 signatures from Manchester, (and 30,000 from Scotland, 7,000 from Bolton) adorned this vain petition which embodied anti-*laissez-faire* (more correctly 'interventionist') ideas.

In April, 1812, Luddism was rampant. Luddites smashed mills near Leeds and Wakefield. A full-scale assault on a mill at Rawfolds in the Spen valley was repulsed by soldiers—this incident was the actual basis of the Luddite attack described in Charlotte Brontë's *Shirley*. In Lancashire and Cheshire the Luddites attacked Manchester, Stockport, Oldham and Rochdale, nearly always heading for mills containing steam looms and dressing machinery. A threatening letter sent to a factory owner ran (spelling corrected): 'In justice to humanity we think it our bounden duty to give you this notice, that is if you do not cause those dressing machines to be removed within . . . seven days, your factory and all that it contains will be set on fire.' The writer insisted that he meant no personal harm

67

to the owner but 'we are fully determined to destroy both dressing machines and steam looms'.

By the autumn of 1812 there were 12,000 troops ranged against Luddism, actual and potential—more than the Duke of Wellington had fighting the armies of Napoleon at the time! Luddism faded out erratically until its last flourish in 1817. It was more than a response to factories, although they were certainly its main cause. Others were the high cost of living, the threat of hunger, the radical politics current since the French Revolution (1789) and a loss of dignity which came with the demise of the domestic system. For all their bravery and desperation, the Luddites backed the most hopeless of causes: nostalgia and anger were powerless before the factory system.

Factories and the Quality of Life

The factory system created much suffering and fear. It had many enemies, such as the hand-loom weavers who risked starvation rather than enter the din and discipline of a factory, whose atmosphere was akin to the 'airless and laughterless life of a prison'. Some factories had an elaborate system of fines and sanctions to intensify discipline. These fines could be a big slice out of wages of 25s. per week:

Leaving window open: 1s. fine
Found dirty at work: 1s.
Washing at work: 1s.
Leaving gaslight on too long: 2s.

Waste left on spindle: 1s.
Off sick, if no replacement available: 6s. per day towards cost of steam engine being kept going uselessly.

These fines were imposed at a Tyldesley (near Manchester) mill. Like its long hours (14 hours a day) these fines were unusually harsh even for the time; on the other hand its 84°F temperature, fluffy atmosphere, intense noise and locked doors were entirely normal.

Each industry had its occupational hazards (see pp. 74–5) and most factory owners resented 'wasting' money on safety devices. Until 1815 Northumberland and Durham did not bother to hold inquests on coal miners killed at work; and even in 1842 the Children's Employment Commission commented on the lethal slackness in safety matters in the pits of the Cumbrian coal magnates: 'when such management is allowed in the mines of two of the most opulent coal proprietors in the kingdom, we cease to wonder at anything that may take place in mines worked equally without capital or science'.

Society was unprepared for the economic revolution based on factories and machines. The new situation seemed in some vague way unnatural. Men were becoming the slaves of machines. Fielden in the *Curse of the Factory System* wrote: 'a steam engine in the hands of an . . . avaricious master is a relentless power to which old and young are equally bound to submit'. The chimneys of Oldham, Dowlais and Shifnal threatened to usher in a new dark age, physically, morally

55 Sheffield, of which J. C. Symons wrote (1845): 'one of the dirtiest and most smoky towns I ever saw'. The proximity of factories to housing added to the squalor of industrial cities as this panorama shows. It also gives a fine impression of the power and scale of industrialism in its age of triumph.

and mentally. A squire wrote (1808): 'the instant we get near the border of the manufacturing parts of Lancashire we meet a fresh race of beings'. Mrs Gaskell spoke (1833) of the factory population as a 'Hercules in the cradle' (a favourite and significant symbol of the era, see p. 40) which, unlike previous societies was 'drawn together into dense masses'.

The suddenness of it all was expressed by W. Cooke Taylor (1843) thus: 'The steam engine has no precedent, the spinning jenny is without ancestry . . . they sprang into sudden existence like Minerva from the brain of Jupiter.' He conveyed a sense of gloom: 'as a stranger passes through the masses of human beings which have accumulated round the mills and print works . . . he cannot contemplate those "crowded hives" without feelings of anxiety . . . almost amounting to dismay . . . there are mighty energies slumbering in these masses'.

The disturbance of William Blake has already been spoken of (p. 13); he wrote of the factory toilers more specifically foretelling that the new system would:

'*bind to labour*
Of day and night the myriads of Eternity that they might file and polish brass and iron
hour after hour laborious workmanship'

The new system was not, however, without its objective friends. One pressure group which lauded it was the Society for the Diffusion of Useful Knowledge, satirised by the novelist, Thomas Love Peacock, as the 'Steam Intellect Society', in an attempt to expose its (to him) crass materialism. Yet the pro-factory men had some valid points, two in particular: factories were here to stay, and they brought much good as well as evil. Dr Ure (1836) thought a factory 'involves the idea of a vast automaton . . . acting in uninterrupted concert for the production of a common object' (a prolix reference to team spirit); and that the factory system was 'a great minister of civilisation to the terraqueous globe'. In their desire to praise and explain the new system the apologists sometimes went too far. As Peacock pointed out, Ure's worship of Arkwright as 'a man of Napoleonic nerve who crushed the refractory tempers of workpeople accustomed to irregular diligence', and fearsome chapter headings in his works such as 'Moral Economy of the Factory System' were austere, unsympathetic and pompous.

The Factory Acts

Growing opposition to many methods associated with the Factory system arose from the early nineteenth century. It was a mixed bag of strange interests containing humanitarians like Lord Shaftesbury, who simply felt that the exploitation of women and children was wrong. There were humane factory owners, who believed in the system, but not its abuse, like Robert Owen who ran his mills on enlightened lines and looked forward to a time when the workers might own their own factories, in a co-operative system. Other humane industrialists were: John Wood of Bradford who gave £40,000 towards the factory law campaign, and Fielden whose factories were among the largest in the world.

Some more cynical factory owners supported the campaign because they hoped that their smaller and poorer competitors would be forced out of business if Parliament ordered shorter hours. Many of the factory workers themselves were to be found on the various committees that pressed for reform, although they insisted that better conditions should not be an excuse for lowering wages. Finally there were the powerful landowners and gentry: they had no love for the 'infant Hercules' of industrialism, which they feared would grow to overwhelm them— as it did. They, and the reforming 'radical' M.P.s, supplied invaluable political support for the movement to humanise the factory system.

The opposition to the proposed laws was formidable. It was supported by many leading economists of the day, who treated *laissez-faire* as Holy Writ and claimed that if hours were shortened or wages raised, foreign competition would defeat Britain by employing cheaper labour. Lord Macaulay (1846) countered this familiar argument thus: 'You try to frighten us by telling us that in some German factories the young work seventeen hours in twenty-four, that . . . there is not one grows to such stature that he can be admitted into the army. . . . Sir, I laugh at the thought of such competition . . . we shall yield . . . not to a race of degenerate dwarfs, but to some people . . . vigorous in body and mind.' The economist, Nassau Senior, produced the argument that factories made profits only in the last hour of the working day; cut the day and economic ruin would follow.

The millowners' allies, e.g. Lord Lauderdale, produced doctors friendly to their cause, and men who claimed that factory discipline moulded 'early subordination, industry and regularity'. Parliament was not frightened or impressed by such claims. Rather it believed the evidence and facts of official enquiries, such as that submitted by the father of two mill girls (1833):

Q: At what time did those girls go to work?

A: In the 'brisk time' (trade good) . . . at 3 o'clock in the morning, and ended at ten at night.

Q: Had any of them any accident in consequence of this labour?

A: Yes, my eldest daughter: the cog caught her forefinger nail . . . and she was five weeks in Leeds Infirmary.

Q: What were her wages in the 'brisk time'?

A: 3s. per week.

It was calm enquiry and deliberation that won the day. Extreme posturing by humanitarians and millowners did the truth little service, although it brought the debate into the political arena. It will be convenient to tabulate the various enquiries and legislation for the sake of brevity, but first the major acts require fuller comment.

The Health and Morals of Apprentices Act, 1802, largely the work of Sir Robert Peel the Elder (father of the Prime Minister), was an attempt to stop the brutal exploitation of factory apprentices. They were to have a twelve-hour day, no night work, clothes and schooling supplied by their employer who also had to 'whitewash the factory twice per year' and see that his charges attended church once a month. The factories employing apprentices had to be registered with the local clerk of the peace. The hours-of-work order applied strictly to apprentices, but certain other clauses to any cotton or wool factory where 'twenty or more persons' worked. The Act failed mainly because the apprentice system was being replaced by child labour, rather than because the magistrates lacked diligence, an explanation occasionally offered.

Factory Act 1819 derived from a proposal of Peel the Elder (1815), aided by Robert Owen, to extend the principles of 1802 to the factory child-labourer. The bill waded through three years of committee investigation, while doctors summoned by both sides argued about the beneficial effects of factory life. The 1818 committee supported the millowners, the 1819 did not. It finally escaped further mauling and became law in 1819: stating (in respect of cotton mills only) that no children under 9 were to be employed: 9 to 16 years old had a twelve-hour maximum day. Many mills gave better conditions than this Act ordered, and its failure to appoint inspectors meant that the law was frequently flouted. John Cam Hobhouse, M.P. said (1825) there had been only two prosecutions under the Act!

Factory Act, 1833   This law was an historic landmark. By giving it 'teeth' in the form of inspectors to enforce it, Parliament implicitly announced that *laissez-faire* was not the supreme economic law of the land, and that limits were to be imposed on the behaviour of factory owners. The terms of the Act were: all textile mills (except silk mills) to be affected, children 9 to 13 years old not to work more than nine hours a day (or 48 hours a week); two hours a day to be devoted to schooling; 'young persons' (13 to 18 years old) to have a twelve-hour day, and, above all, four inspectors were appointed.

H.M. Inspectors of Factories   The governing party of 1833, the Whigs, appointed four loyal supporters to these posts worth £1,000 a year, an example of the patronage still quite common before the Civil Service reforms (1859–70). However, very capable men were chosen who would be needed to deal with the hostile and crafty factory owners. They were given 3,000 factories to inspect, and allowed to appoint sub-inspectors (at about £300 a year) to help them. If the inspectors found erring factory owners they were to prosecute them, a sanction which made this Act meaningful, unlike the damp squibs of 1802 and 1815. The Inspectors also produced reports on their work, which are a rich store of factory history, probably the oldest and fullest in the world. In later years various specialist inspectors have been appointed under other legislation to watch particularly dangerous industries, e.g. the Electrical Inspectors, various Medical Inspectors and Alkali Inspectors. Their work has grown as the factory system, and its relevant laws, have both spread.

Year	Number of Inspectors	No. of factories to be inspected
1833	4	3,154
1964	517	225,000

In addition to inspecting factories 'textile and non-textile' as they are still sometimes described, the factory inspectors report on other places of work, e.g. docks, power stations and certain offices.

The Ten Hours Movement and the Factory Act, 1847   Although the philosophy of *laissez-faire* had failed to stop the 1833 Act, the factory owners were able to put up a dogged resistance to other hopeful reforms. The greatest of these was the

56 The sweating system: Russian exiles toiling under harsh conditions in London's East End in the early twentieth century. The system was opposed by humanitarian pressure groups (such as the bizarrely named 'Anti Sweating League') and duly undermined by the Trade Boards Act, 1909.

so-called 'Ten Hours Movement', which wanted a ten-hour maximum working day for all. The pressure groups organised to educate parliament and the public in the matter were known as 'Short Time Committees'. Working class members of these committees wanted the ten-hour day for all, including men, but the bulk of the movement were not willing to go that far. Women and children needed protection, but not men, who were (theoretically) able to fight and bargain for decent wages and conditions as free citizens.

The movement started in Lancashire in 1825, and enlisted the predictable opposition to capitalist excess. A contemporary newspaper (*Leeds Mercury*, 1844) called the committees 'a strange combination of Socialists, Chartists and Ultra Tories'—specifically the leaders were: Lord Shaftesbury (then Lord Ashley); John Doherty (a trade unionist, general secretary of the Federation of Cotton Spinners); Fielden, the rich factory owner, and Lord John Manners, a Tory romantic (see p. 14) who saw the factory system as a deadly threat to the old landowner-dominated England that he pined for—a strange combination indeed!

The 1833 Act excited some hostility from parts of the movement because it allowed a factory to employ two separate shifts of child labour, each of eight hours. This meant a possible sixteen-hour working day for adult members of the factory staff. The agitation for a ten-hour working day for all textile workers intensified in the early 1840s. The main tactic employed was to urge a limit on the hours of female labour, the pillar of textile production. The case of the reformers was strengthened by the report of the Children's Employment Commission, 1843, which showed that the controversial last hour of work, far from making a profit, was usually performed by tired and inefficient labour, the cause of financial loss, not gain. The struggle reached a climax 1844–47; first a twelve-hour bill was obtained (1844) and at last a ten-hour bill (1847), which became the *Factory Act, 1847*, sometimes called the *Ten Hour Act*.

There was to be a finale to the heroic age of factory law. When the 1847 Act was passed it was greeted joyfully in the textile districts. This euphoria evaporated when millowners evaded the spirit of the law by employing child and female labour in shifts but keeping the adult men working long and hard hours. One of the great objectives of the 1847 Act seemed to be neutralised, especially when Baron Parke, a judge of the Court of Exchequer, pronounced that this 'relay system' was technically legal (1849). The confusion was ended by the Factory Act, 1850, which laid down a definite working day of $10\frac{1}{2}$ hours, not quite what the committees had wanted, but very near.

Industry and Accidents

The factory system brought many occupational hazards and ailments, which the State has sought to avert over the years, usually with the help of the employers. Industrial disease was much older than the factory system; for instance, the dreaded mining disease *pneumoconiosis* (which results from breathing coal dust into the lungs) is as old as coal mining, and 'industrial accidents' could easily happen in a mediaeval carpentery shop, or in a Carthaginian shipyard. The factory system caused a sharp rise in these hazards to health, partly because it increased industrial activity, and partly because it introduced new and often dangerous methods of production.

Gruesome names were given to the new industrial diseases of the factory age: factory fever, grinder's rot, phossy jaw and slateworker's lung. Medical research uncovered their secrets and they have usually been mastered by prevention, and in many cases, cure.

Some factory conditions did not directly cause illness, but rendered it more likely; for instance the badly ventilated cotton mills, thick with flying fluff, sharply increased the incidence of pneumonia, a disease of the lungs. People who worked in an atmosphere of stone dust (flint grinders, quarrymen, miners digging through rock, cutlery-grinders) might well contract *silicosis*, another lung infection which was known by various horrific trade names, mentioned above. Improved methods of production often exacerbated the problem—for instance blasting mines with dynamite and using pneumatic drills threw up greater volumes of dust.

The pioneer of industrial medicine was the Leeds doctor Charles Thackrah

(1795–1832), who wrote the first modern work on the subject in 1831. In this he noted the evil effects of long hours, awkward posture and foul atmosphere upon workers, and he equated lung disease with certain conditions already alluded to. For instance, he wrote: 'Dr Knight in the North of England Medical journal states that fork grinders who use a dry grindstone die at the age of 28 or 32, while the table knife grinders who work on wet stone survive to between 40 and 50.'

The question of safety in factories and mines occupied early reformers as much as health. The *Factory Act 1844* ordered textile factory owners to encase shafting (long rods transmitting power from steam engines to mules and looms). The millowners did this with reluctance, and fought the law then and later with various organisations such as the Factory Law Amendment Association, and the National Association of Factory Occupiers, castigated by Charles Dickens as the 'Association for the Mangling of Operatives'. The factory owners lost: the law was not modified, but intensified, e.g. the *Factory Act 1864* which ordered that 'every factory to which this Act applies' should be kept as 'harmless so far as is practicable'. The third Commission on Children's Employment (1863–67) revealed many shocking conditions existing in factories not yet covered by the law, which still largely applied to mines and textile mills only. Such additional factories that had been included up to the 1860s were closely related to the textile mills: textile printing works (1845); bleaching and dyeing works (1860); lace works (1861).

The report on the pottery industry, for instance, made grim reading, stating that: 'each successive generation of potters becomes more dwarfed and less robust than the preceding one', and observed that children had to dart into vast stoves heated to 140°F. Children in match-factories were likely to contract phossy jaw (*necrosis* of the jawbone) which could lead to disfigurement or death and was always acutely painful. The law based on these reports protected women and children from the more dangerous occupations (*Factory Act 1864, Factory Act Extension Act 1867*).

The 1860s also saw the law extending beyond obvious factories to workshops (defined as places where less than 50 people were employed in manufacture), e.g. *Workshops Act 1867*. The last major extensions in factory law were the *Trade Boards Act 1909* (**56**) and the 'office workers' charter', the *Offices, Shops and Railway Premises Act 1963* which gave many 'white-collar workers' the protection afforded to industrial workers much earlier.

Factories and the State: A Summary

In 1809 Parliament was scrapping the old Elizabethan economic laws; a century later it maintained a complex series of codes and regulations to control factory and industrial life. *Laissez-faire* may have been popular with certain interests, but it was never unchallenged for long. It was once called the 'only untried utopia', fortunately perhaps, for the historian, Arnold Toynbee, trembled 'to think what this country would have been but for the Factory Acts'.

The influence of pressure groups was important in getting factory law placed on the statute book: Short Time Committees, trade unions, etc. They are now an accepted feature of modern democracies and early industrial problems supplied much of their basis. As late as 1900 no factory law actually regulated the hours of male adults. It is still the case that wages and conditions for male workers are mostly thrashed out by negotiation between employers and employees, usually represented by their trade unions—what is termed 'collective bargaining'. In some industries these matters are settled by *Wages Councils*, descendants of the Trade Boards set up by the 1909 Act. These are government sponsored and so a part of the elaborate State supervisory apparatus dating from 1802.

Factory Law: a chronology and summary

Act or investigation	Date	Terms
Health and Morals of Apprentices Act	1802	Textile mills only, dealt with 'Poor Law' Apprentices only
Peel's Committee, and House of Lord's Committee	1815–19	Investigated child labour
Cotton Mills & Factories Act	1819	12-hour day for children in textile mills
Factory Act	1831	No night work below age 21
1st Report on Children's Employment	1833	Basis for 1833 Act, Second Report 1843
Factory Act	1833	H.M. Inspectors, etc.
Factory Act	1844	12-hour Act, machinery to be fenced
Factory Act	1847	10-hour Act
Factory Act	1850	Enforced spirit of 1847 Act
Commission on bleach and dye works	1854	Investigated
Bleach & Dye Works Act	1860	Extended law
RC on Children's Employment (Third)	1862–66	
Alkali Act	1863	Attacked air and river pollution
Factory Act Factory Act Extension Act	1864 1867	Law extended to non-textile factories
Workshop Act	1867	Extended law, no children under 8 to be employed anywhere
Factory Act	1874	No children under 10 to be employed
Factory Act	1878	Repealed old laws and re-enacted them clearly; said to 'codify' law

Act or investigation	Date	Terms
Employers' Liability Act	1880	Employers to pay for certain industrial accidents
Cotton Cloth Factory Act	1889	Regulates atmosphere in textile mills
Factory Act	1891	Minimum age 11
Factory Act	1895	Docks and laundries added
Shop Hours Act	1895	State protection widens beyond factories
Factory and Workshops Consolidation Act	1901	Another big codification: adds electric power stations
Alkali Act	1906	Present law, covers 2,000 works
Coal Mines Acts	1908⎱ 1912⎰	Minimum wages fixed
Trade Boards Act	1909	Attacks 'sweating', covers 3 million unprotected workers in small works, etc.
Factory Act	1937	Abolishes old distinction between textile and non-textile factories and workshops. Minister of Labour allowed to make special regulations for different industries
Mines & Quarries Act	1954	Nobody under 16 to work underground
Clean Air Act	1956	Attacks air pollution; by 1966 factories responsible for only one quarter of all smoke (total: 1·2 million tons of smoke, 800,000 tons of grit and 6·7 million tons of sulphur dioxide p.a!)
Factory Act	1961	Consolidates previous law, the 'last word'
Offices, Shops & Railway Premises Act	1963	Extends spirit of factory law well beyond world of mills, docks, etc., and covers 8 million people

Full, but very technical, information on all factory law can be found in *Redgrave's Factory Acts*, which has now run to twenty editions.

In addition to the Acts listed, which provide the framework of factory law, there are many leading cases in law on the subject, and certain Ministers of the crown are allowed to make special regulations under the terms of various Acts, a process known as 'delegated legislation'.

Factories and the People

The reaction of society as a whole to the factory system went far beyond Luddism and the Factory Acts. There were multitudes of responses to the fact of mills, ironworks and industrial cities: political, aesthetic, philosophical and religious. Some examples will show the immense diversity of this social reaction. Mention has already been made of Robert Owen's challenge to capitalism: co-operation. This was tried from time to time in the Industrial Revolution, but enjoyed indifferent success beside the much more successful co-operative retailing movement (1844 onwards)—still strong. Some co-operatively-owned cotton mills flourished in the 1860s, and a variation known as the 'Oldham Limiteds' (mid-1870s) has received much attention and comment in economic history.

A political by-product of the early factory era was Chartism. This was a movement of the late 1830s and the 1840s which demanded full democracy. The working class had high hopes of its succeeding, although its objectives were actually gained long after its demise. It received some support from the new manufacturing towns, but much more from those which had been hit by the spread of the factories elsewhere, e.g. the old West Country cloth centres like Trowbridge, or villages where domestic industry was making a last forlorn stand in the face of the factories. The environs of Barnsley and Nottingham (and remote villages in the Pennines) contained many such workers, and had names which reflected the desperation of their inhabitants: Beggarinton, Slave Row, Hunger Hill, etc. (E. M. Sigworth).

57 The omnipresent factory: a scene at Oldham, Lancashire (Featherstone Road and Main Road) showing textile mills dominating streets of tenement housing. The water in 'lodges' is for the steam engines which drove the mills.

58 Trafford Park Estate: the world's first trading estate (1897) seen here in 1903 as workers stream out of the electrical works of the British Westinghouse Co. (now G.E.C.-A.E.I.). The estate covers 1,200 acres, contains 200 factories and gives work to 50,000 people. The eminent success of this industrial 'complex' encouraged the building of others (**63**), its main attraction being readily available land, power, and bulk transport: all vital for large-scale factory production.

Towns which were untroubled by poverty-stricken hand-loom weavers showed no enthusiasm for the movement; for instance, the new iron, railway and engineering centres. A recent work states that 'the factory workers were less ardent', and writers of the time noted 'their revulsion from . . . an appeal to physical force'. Chartism, like Luddism, had many more origins than the arrival of the factories, although fear of them, and the helpless despair they engendered were powerful elements in sustaining it.

One hardy and successful product of the working class reaction to industrialism was the *Trade Union*, a society dedicated to gaining better wages and conditions for its members, and also acting as a 'Friendly Society' in which members subscribed towards pensions, sickness benefits, etc.

In many cases factories were built in or near existing towns, and the resulting congestion and squalor was acute (**55**). There are many records of this, for instance Dr Robertson (1840) talking of Manchester and Salford (population then 260,000): 'The factories have necessarily sprung up along the watercourses which are the Irk, Irwell and Medlock, and the Rochdale Canal . . . new streets are rapidly extending in every direction and so great already is the expanse of the towns, that those who live in the more populous quarters can seldom hope to see the green face of nature.' The first of many generations was being born that would not know the countryside; only with the leisure and mass-transport of the twentieth century were they released from these industrial fortresses. Modern town planning tries to avoid the solid urban area of 'back to back' houses found in the past.

Yet many of the new industrial cities were very proud and progressive in civic matters. They erected splendid public buildings, like Leeds Town Hall, organised police, fire services, gas and water supplies for the citizens. The heavy dependence on coal as a source of energy meant that houses and factories made these great cities very dirty: their grime became legendary, and pseudo-aesthetes still affect a shudder of horror at the thought of Halifax in the rain. For all their dirt, however, the factory cities had grandeur, pride and genuine comradeship—probably more than modern suburbs.

Certain distinctive types of factories were constructed to serve these cities and their mills with light and power, for instance the gasworks of over 1,000 under-takings, power stations and waterworks. Factory methods were employed in these from the beginning, indeed, early gasworks were called 'gas factories'.

One palpable change of the twentieth century has been the gradual separation of living quarters from the factory area of industrial towns. It was the rule in Victorian times and earlier to live under the shadow of the factory which gave one work (57); today many people travel to work by 'bus, train or in their own cars. The development in transport techniques has made possible the erection of large suburbs, and the concentration of factories on special estates (58) (64).

By 1914 society bore the distinctive stamp of the factory system in many ways.

59 The new industrial towns broke with the tradition of using local building materials. Large-scale brickmaking and slate quarrying were possible at the source of raw materials because of bulk transport available by railways: the remote ancestor of 'industrialised building', i.e. pre-fabricated houses. Here is the giant Delabole Quarry, St Teath, North Cornwall, a mechanised excavation 400 feet deep and said to be one of the largest man-made holes on earth. Note the water-wheel, tramways and steam cranes.

60 shows the mechanical trimming of roof slates.

People bought, ate, travelled in and wore its products. Of the total population (*c*. 40 millions) over 1 million worked in coal mines, and the same in textile mills; another 1½ millions in engineering works. The more obvious manifestations of the factories were there for all to see: the forests of factory chimneys, smoking obelisks of the industrial age. Other aspects were more subtle, for instance the way of life of millions of people was dominated by factory hours—a fact they accepted as 'normal', although such regimentation had been unknown for all but a fraction of human history. Men and women often worked in shifts, a series of waves designed to cover a long period in which the expensive factory machinery could run continuously and so earn its keep.

In some areas an entire town might go on holiday at once, so that mutually dependent factories and families were not left without associates; for instance the famous Lancashire *Wakes Week*. There was an orchestra of factory noises: the hooter (another example of the time-domination of the system) which summoned shifts from the surrounding streets; the crash of hammers and the beat of engines. The novelist, J. B. Priestley, has stated that a peculiarity of certain Yorkshire dialects (mainly West Riding) has its origin in the clatter and din of the mills: the habit of repeating sentences for the sake of clarity, thus: 'A nice day today; I say a nice day today.' Factories bred their own jargon and humour, much of which is now accepted idiom: 'clocking in', 'overtime', even 'trouble up 't mill' uttered by people who may never have been North of the Thames!

The connexion between the factory system and morality, or lack of it, has aroused many debates. The ferocious drinking of many people in the nineteenth century has been explained as their reaction to the drudgery of the factory world. A writer said of Leeds (1845): 'the feelings of the people are blunted . . . from the constantly contaminated state of the atmosphere . . . leading to listlessness and inducing a desire for spirits and opiates.' A grim phrase put it more bluntly: 'the quickest way out of Manchester is in a bottle'. In point of fact it is hard to prove direct connexion between industrialism and intemperance, a vice which has afflicted many societies that were devoid of a factory system.

Similarly, the question of industrialism and its links with religious fervour has vexed many minds. Writers like Marx, Engels and George Bernard Shaw have argued that religion was the 'opium of the masses' encouraged by factory owners to render workers docile. Others have pointed out the association of early Methodism and trade unionism. The numbers of devout and church-going factory workers was a good deal less than is generally supposed.

In short, one must distinguish between those obvious and provable links between factories and society; and supposed ones, which, although interesting to debate, remain largely hypothetical. In the only religious census taken in Britain (on a Sunday in 1851) very few industrial workers attended any religious service. It has been said that 'the poor, at least in the great towns, were largely pagan, with a veneer of religious observation and much hidden superstition'. It was the middle class of factory owners and managers, of clerks and technicians who supplied the main link between the new industrialism and religion, and, of course, the immense numbers of Irish Catholics who settled in Manchester, Liverpool and Glasgow to provide a large proportion of the working class in the early factory age.

61 *Modern Times*: Charlie Chaplin's classic film (1936) which questioned some values of the factory age; production for its own sake, men dwarfed by machinery and factories as an end, not a means. Many attempts have been made to counteract the tedium of factory work, especially by industrial psychologists (1920 onwards).

62 Industry and Domesday: *The Great Day of His Wrath*, an apocalyptic oil painting by John Martin (1855), one of 'the most sublime and extraordinary pictures in the World', shows the end of the world, with tumbling mountains, a yawning and fiery abyss, helpless multitudes swept away in terror. The source is partly the *Revelation (VI)*, partly a night journey through the Black Country: 'the glow of the furnaces, the red blaze of light . . . seemed to his mind truly sublime and awful. He could not imagine anything more terrible even in regions of everlasting punishment'. So said the artist's son, Leopold, suggesting that his father was amongst those who feared the force of industrialism which man had created.

Factories and the Arts

There were three phases of literary and artistic reaction to the factory age. First came wonder; the poems of Erasmus Darwin and the paintings of Joseph Wright of Derby (**17**). Then came doubt, shading, finally into horror and hostility. One section of the *literati* has remained opposed to industrialism; another has, in this century, accepted and used it as a background for paintings (e.g. C. S. Lowry's 'factoryscapes') and literature (Llewellyn's *How Green Was My Valley*; Sillitoe's *Saturday Night and Sunday Morning*; D. H. Lawrence's *Sons and Lovers*).

In the first, 'honeymoon' period, one finds that the Rev. J. Dalton addressing *Two Ladies on their Returning from Viewing the Mines at Whitehaven* (1755), waxes enthusiastic:

> *. . . loftier chambers of the deep,*
> *Whose jetty pillars seem to groan*
> *Beneath a ponderous roof of stone.*
> *Then with increasing wonder gaze*
> *The dark inextricable maze*
> *Where cavern crossing cavern meets*
> *(City of subterranean streets!)*

83

and Erasmus Darwin who sang the praises of machinery in his *Botanic Garden* (1789–91), in this case a beam engine:

> *. . . the piston falls*
> *Restless sliding through its iron walls;*
> *Quick moves the balanced beam, of giant birth*
> *Wields his large limbs, and nodding shakes the earth.*

Lesser poets caught this enthusiasm, for instance J. Bisset's *Poetic Survey round Birmingham* (1800):

> *Soho! Where Genius and the Arts preside*
> *Europe's wonder and Britannia's pride.*

and Erasmus Darwin's friend, Anna Seward, the Swan of Lichfield:

> *Grim Wolverhampton lights her smouldering fires*
> *And Sheffield, smoke involved, dim where she stands*
> *Circled by lofty mountains . . .*

However, another woman writer, somewhat later, expressed a different reaction to the march of technology. This was Mary Shelley (wife of the poet), who wrote *Frankenstein* (1817), an allegory of industrialism, whereby a clever physician creates a monster which runs out of control. The implicit question was, would industrialism destroy civilisation? The painter, John Martin, became obsessed with the idea of a fiery cataclysm (**62**) which Dickens also described in one of his rare excursions into industrial subjects: 'But night-time in this dreadful spot!—night when the smoke was changed to fire, when every chimney spirted up its flame . . . when the noise of every strange machine was aggravated by the darkness' (*Little Nell*, 1841) and Birmingham: 'the whirl of wheels and noise of machinery shook the trembling walls. The fires whose lurid sullen light had been visible for miles blazed fiercely up in the great works and factories of the town' (*Pickwick Papers*, 1837).

Matthew Arnold (son of the headmaster of Rugby (see p. 6) did not share his father's sanguine approach to industrialism, which he feared was creating a new barbarism: 'Faith in machinery is our besetting danger' he warned. Benjamin Disraeli, statesman and novelist, wrote *Sybil* (1845), in which he made his famous distinction between the 'two Englands'—the rich and the poor—which were separate and hostile.

Yet the most remarkable thing about industrial life and great literature is the absence of links; a fact of considerable significance. Many great novelists of the nineteenth and twentieth centuries hardly touched on factories or mills or mines in their works at all: Thackeray, Trollope, Scott, Maugham and the Brontës. A few did, for instance Arnold Bennett and D. H. Lawrence, but they, unlike the general run of writers, knew industrialism at first hand. In spite of factories and mines being the basis of the nation's economic life, and the background to millions of lives, there remained large sections of the population who knew little of these things, and usually regretted even that. A strong body of intellectuals still remains concerned about the ill effects of the factories on society, and persists in the belief that times were better before the mills; a spirit enshrined in the ideas of William Morris, who dreamed in the *Earthly Paradise* (1868):

> *Forget six counties overhung with smoke*
> *Forget the snorting steam and piston stroke*
> *. . . Think rather of the pack horse on the down*
> *And dream of London small and white and clean   . . . .*
> *The clear Thames bordered by its gardens clean.*

This is a convenient point to look at the nineteenth-century factory system in perspective. The escapism of Morris reminded people of a (then) not so remote pre-industrial world. The factors of which they complained—dirt, noise, poverty, grinding toil were products of their age, not inherent parts of the factory system. There are no evils endemic in factory production. The state of technology, the reliance on coal, the low efficiency of labour (and hence its meagre rewards) were factors of the age. One day many factories may be unmanned; already improved machinery, shorter hours and numerous 'fringe benefits' (canteens, recreation rooms, etc.) of many factories are creating a different kind of civilisation from the smoky inferno associated with nineteenth-century Rotherham or Elswick. 'Carboniferous capitalism' was a stage that had to be endured *en route* to a far higher standard of living—for all—than any nineteenth-century Utopian ever dreamed of.

Reading List

F. C. Klingender: *Art and the Industrial Revolution*
F. C. Mather: *Chartism*
Eric Sigworth: *The Black Dyke Mills*
Eric Thompson: *The Rise of the English Working Class*
G. D. H. Cole and Raymond Postgate: *The Common People 1746–1938*

5 The Factory System in the Twentieth Century

In 1914 about a quarter of the working population worked in factories. If mining and agriculture were added, the proportion rose to 40%. In 1969, the proportion is 43%. This apparent similarity masks some important developments: the working population is much larger in 1969 (24 millions against 18 millions) and the output per factory worker is far greater—hence the factory system itself is more widespread and efficient than it was before the Great War. It is entirely possible that the number employed in factories will fall in the future as automation spreads. However, unmanned factories are factories still, and the system shows no signs of weakening, nor has it now any viable rivals. The rest of the working population is in the 'service industries' or government service—it is highly likely that these sources of employment will grow because they are hard to mechanise and automate. They are the last, and very strong fortress, of the 'personal touch'.

Within the statistics below there lies a long tale of industrial change which has occurred in the last forty years: coal and cotton (the 'old staples') have declined, and new industries, like chemicals and motor vehicle manufacture, have been created. In the 1920s and 1930s there was high unemployment in the old staples, and not a few other industries, e.g. engineering, shipbuilding and steel-making.

This period of the 'depression' or 'slump' finally buried the doctrine of *laissez-faire*. With 75% of the men out of work in some towns, for instance Merthyr Tydfil, it was no longer possible to argue that a 'hidden or invisible hand' was at work adjusting the economy for the good of all. The new school of economic

63 A price of factory civilisation unknown in agrarian society: mass unemployment. Here men search for work at a Labour Exchange in 1939, a year in which two million people (12% of the working population then) were out of work.

thought, led by Lord Keynes, advocated State spending and help, a process to cure the economic ills of the time. While the economy as a whole could be helped, the old staples had a grim future and lost business and workers beyond recall.

Percentage distribution of workers between the wars

	% 1918	% 1938
Textiles	20	15
Engineering	15	18·2
Vehicles	5·8	9·2

Old Staples and New Industries

A representative sample of new factory products in this century would be: cars and lorries, electric power, consumer durables (washing machines, TV sets, vacuum cleaners, etc.), the cinema (**65**), and the mass-produced 'national daily' newspapers. These and other products have generally experienced growing markets.

Why did the old staples decline? There were four reasons. Foreign rivals set up their own textile mills and had their own industrial revolutions; world trade was sluggish between the wars; substitutes appeared (oil and hydro-electricity for Britain's overseas coal markets; man-made fibres for cotton textiles) and, in more recent years, the State has been unwilling to prop up declining industries indefinitely. Instead it has planned their run-down on fairly generous terms.

One of the hardiest new industries has been the generation of electricity (**66**, **67**, **68**). The generating stations which appeared in Britain from the late nineteenth century onwards were an extension of the factory system. The public welcomed this new source of power for domestic and industrial use. Markets grew fast:

Year	Number of consumers of electricity
1920	730,000
1929	2,844,000
1938	8,920,000
1968	20,000,000

and bulk supplies of raw material (coal and oil) were available to feed the power stations. Generally speaking, the larger a power station is, the more efficient it becomes. Because of restrictive laws, Britain was slow to encourage a pattern of few and immense power stations: in 1925 there were 28 large stations generating half of Britain's electricity, but another 322 producing only 11% of the total power. In order to create the necessary pattern, the State arranged a 'national grid' (1926) of pylon-borne transmission lines.

64 *(left)* The Solway Trading Estate at Maryport, Cumberland, was built under the Special Areas Act (1936) as an early and modest attempt to relieve unemployment in a declining coal port. Now, the estate makes, *inter alia*, children's wear and precision instruments. **65** *(right)* Mass entertainment: by the application of factory methods and capital investment the 'productivity' of actors is now far higher. They are seen by millions on cinema or television screens. Cinemas date from the early twentieth century; 'super cinemas' (like the Odeon, Kingstanding, Birmingham, designed by H. W. Weedon, 1935) date from the inter-war years. Around 1948 there were 4,500 cinemas, admitting 1,000 million people a year. The number both of cinemas and patrons is less now because of the competition from television.

This has had many consequences. The pylons altered the appearance of much of rural Britain: a reminder, even in remote parts, that Britain has now a factory-based economy. The grid enabled electrified factories to be built virtually anywhere. The location of industry was released at a stroke from the domination of 'King Coal', and industry, especially light industry, began to move South to the big markets of London and the Home Counties. The factory towns of the twentieth century have been Slough, Luton and Dagenham. While these growth points flourished in the 1930s, the old staple centres languished. Jarrow, a shipbuilding town in County Durham had an unemployment rate of 75%; Bedfordshire but 6%. While the markets for ships and coal were poor, that for electric engineering was good; it employed 173,000 in 1924 and 367,000 in 1937. An even more startling growth rate was obtained in the vehicle industry. In 1913 some 34,000 motor vehicles were made in Britain, the majority were hand-made and expensive. Some four years earlier, the American, Henry Ford, had shown that it was possible to mass-produce cars, like cotton textiles, by the intense division of

Three ages of electricity supply. **66** *(top right)* shows the interior of Canterbury Corporation power station (1899), a small-scale local works (4·3 MW capacity) with delicate architecture and baroque machinery. **67** *(middle right)* The huge and functional Brighton A station (1906) of Brighton Corporation, seen in later years (190 MW capacity) and built to receive bulk supplies of coal by sea. **68** *(bottom right)* The nuclear-powered Dungeness A of the Central Electricity Generating Board (550 MW capacity) which commenced working in 1965. The advantages of large-scale generation were obtained after nationalisation (1948) which speeded the demise of such stations as **66**, closed in 1959.

labour and widespread standardisation. He was emulated (1921) by the Englishman, Herbert Austin, who started to mass-produce cars in Birmingham; the famous 'Austin 7'. Shortly after he was followed by William Morris (later Lord Nuffield) and by 1925 these two men were making 41% of Britain's standard cars (**70**).

The mass-production of motor vehicles is, perhaps, one of the factory system's greatest triumphs, in that it blossomed into a major industry in less than ten years. The usual elements encouraged factory production, in particular, the existence of big markets. Mass-production made a car cheaper to build than the old craft methods; therefore more people were able to buy the car and markets grew. Bigger and more efficient factories lowered costs further (referred to as the 'economies of scale').

	1923	*1937*
Motor vehicles manufactured:	95,000	511,000
Numbers employed making them:	220,000	380,000
Cost of producing one car	£259	£130

The motor-car industry was the first modern industry to mass-produce 'consumer durables'. This portentous phrase merely means things bought by customers (cars, refrigerators, furniture) which last, rather than those which quickly get consumed or perish (cabbages, sweets, cigarettes). However, like Richard Arkwright, modern businessmen require big and growing markets to justify this factory investment. One leading economist has stated that this objective of 'growth above all' is the main feature of big business today.

69 Modern factories: the Glacier Metal Co.'s works at Alperton, Middlesex, is typical of southern industry. West of London, between the wars, a large industrial belt grew up, supplied by road and powered by electricity. Compare with, say, **57**.

70 Early mass production of motor-cars; in this case the Morris 8 *h.p.* standard car (1929). The great scale of the motor-car markets enables vehicle manufacturers to erect fully integrated works (cf. **71**).

The Future

During the Industrial Revolution, when South Wales and Lancashire were the new Golconda, the Sussex iron industry and West Country wool trade were declining. The future lay, it seemed in the North. In 1890, H. de B. Gibbins could claim that 'the vast majority of the working population is now found North of the Trent'. In 1969 the bulk of the working population is South of that river. The wheel has turned nearly full circle (**72**) and Britain's future factories are just as likely to be associated with Kent or Essex as they were once with Yorkshire and Clydeside. (**69**)

It is almost certain that factory methods will be applied to all manufacturing, and many service industries in the future. Some trades and professions will resist this trend, especially where personal service is especially desired (e.g. shops and hotels), but self-service restaurants (called 'eating factories' by some in their early years, *c.* 1940 onwards) show that no process is really sacred before the burgeoning factory empire if circumstances dictate it. It has been noted that

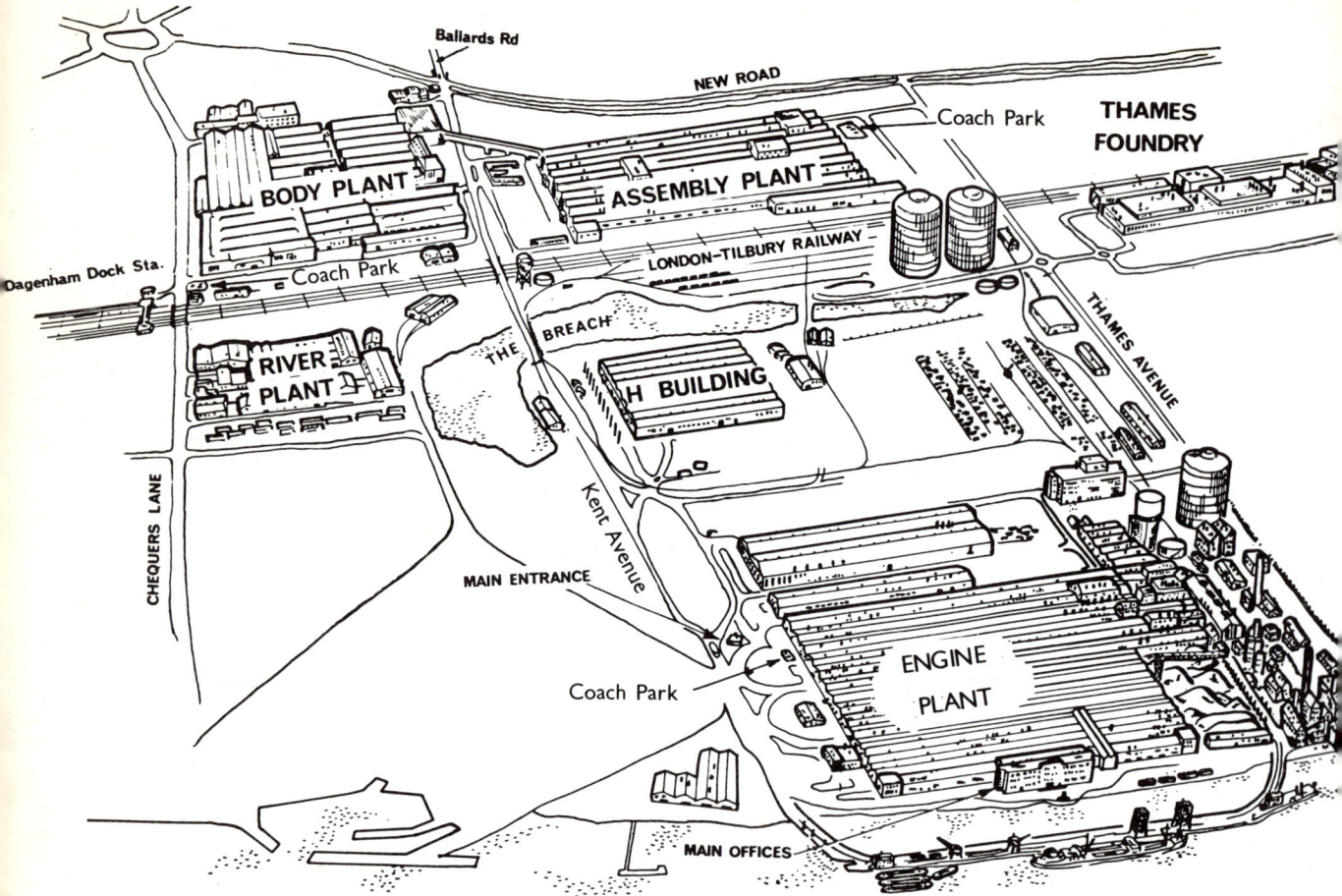

Ballards Rd · NEW ROAD · Coach Park · **THAMES FOUNDRY** · **BODY PLANT** · **ASSEMBLY PLANT** · Dagenham Dock Sta. · Coach Park · LONDON–TILBURY RAILWAY · THAMES AVENUE · THE BREACH · **RIVER PLANT** · **H BUILDING** · CHEQUERS LANE · Kent Avenue · MAIN ENTRANCE · **ENGINE PLANT** · Coach Park · MAIN OFFICES

71 Ford's industrial estate in Essex.

factories may well employ fewer people per factory as automation spreads: this is the heart of the so-called 'second industrial revolution'. The phrase is slightly misleading and contrived, for the essence of the first industrial revolution was to take manufacture from cottages and workshops and put it into factories and this will still be the rule, although they will be operated in new ways. The real 'revolution' occurred in Arkwright's time.

It is likely that the ambivalent attitude of society towards factories will continue: people will regret the passing of home-made cheese and cider, hand-built limousines, and craftsmanship in general. At the same time the needs of a modern and advanced society will be satisfied by mass-production and standardisation alone. The greater efficiency of labour in modern factories has led to higher

72 *(right)* Industry in the south: the Esso oil refinery at Fawley, near Southampton, which covers 1,200 acres and cost over £100 million. The expense and complication of modern factory methods are clear in this works which can produce nearly two million gallons of motor spirit a day. Tankers supply the refinery with $16\frac{1}{2}$ million tons of crude oil a year, mostly from Libya and the Middle East.

wages and less grinding toil. Thus factories, although they supplant handicrafts, raise the standard of living, supply a vast population with its needs and exact less time and energy from factory workers. Long before the factory age, the Greek philosopher, Aristotle (384–322 B C), forecast: 'when looms weave by themselves man's slavery will end'. After its greatest triumphs, the German philosopher Oswald Spengler thought that man had become 'the slave of his creation'. Both are right in their respective ways. There can be genuine hope that sheer drudgery may one day be a thing of the past. Yet civilisation is now utterly dependent on the factory system: domestic industry could not sustain modern society for more than a few weeks.

Reading List
C. L. Mowat: *Britain Between the Wars*
Sidney Pollard: *The Development of the British Economy 1914–1950*

LIVERPOOL COLLEGE OF ART

INDEX

The numerals in **bold type** refer to the figure-numbers of the illustrations

FACTORIES